POLITICAL RESPONSIBILITY REFOCUSED

Thinking Justice after Iris Marion Young

In our highly globalized and networked society, even our most seemingly local actions can have far-reaching social, political, economic, and environmental consequences. Has this changed our moral and political obligations towards people distant from us in space and time – for instance, to generations who are not yet or no longer living, or towards those beyond the borders of our own nations?

Political Responsibility Refocused explores the theoretical foundations and practical implications of individual and collective responsibility towards those who are spatially or temporally separate from us. These essays offer critical assessments of our political responsibilities on topics such as residential schools, sweatshop labour, climate change, and forms of energy generation. Inspired by the final published writings of political and social theorist Iris Marion Young, specifically her outline of a "social connection model" of political responsibility, the contributors assess whether there are practices, policies, and institutions that could meaningfully address these expanded political responsibilities.

GENEVIEVE FUJI JOHNSON is an associate professor in the Department of Political Science at Simon Fraser University.

LORALEA MICHAELIS is an associate professor in the Department of Politics and International Relations at Mount Allison University.

Political Responsibility Refocused

Thinking Justice after
Iris Marion Young

EDITED BY GENEVIEVE FUJI JOHNSON
AND LORALEA MICHAELIS

UNIVERSITY OF TORONTO PRESS
Toronto Buffalo London

ISBN 978-1-4426-4645-2 (cloth)
ISBN 978-1-4426-1442-0 (paper)

∞

Printed on acid-free, 100% post-consumer recycled paper with
vegetable-based inks.

Publication cataloguing information is available from Library
and Archives Canada.

This book has been published with the help of a grant from the Canadian
Federation for the Humanities and Social Sciences, through the Awards
to Scholarly Publications Program, using funds provided by the Social
Sciences and Humanities Research Council of Canada.

University of Toronto Press acknowledges the financial assistance to its
publishing program of the Canada Council for the Arts and the Ontario
Arts Council.

Canada Council   Conseil des Arts
for the Arts   du Canada

ONTARIO ARTS COUNCIL
CONSEIL DES ARTS DE L'ONTARIO
50 YEARS OF ONTARIO GOVERNMENT SUPPORT OF THE ARTS
50 ANS DE SOUTIEN DU GOUVERNEMENT DE L'ONTARIO AUX ARTS

University of Toronto Press acknowledges the financial support of the
Government of Canada through the Canada Book Fund for its publishing
activities.

Contents

Acknowledgments

The idea for this volume arose from a workshop on political responsibility that we organized as part of the Political Theory Section of the 2009 annual general meeting of the Canadian Political Science Association (CPSA). The CPSA program chair, Joseph Wong, had the idea of inviting both Genevieve and Loralea to act as Political Theory Section Heads. We are most grateful to Joe for this foresight. Not only did it spawn a fruitful workshop and most interesting collection of essays, but also a wonderful friendship between the co-editors of this volume. We would like also to thank the original participants of the workshop for their contributions: Howard Adelman, Paul Baxter, Neil Hibbert, Nancy Kokaz, Ingrid Makus, Margaret Moore, Adrian Neer, Tanja Pritzlaff, J.L. Schiff, Daniel Weinstock, Melissa Williams, Catherine Lu, and Ed Andrew.

For ably shepherding the volume from its beginnings through to its completion, we thank University of Toronto Press editor, Daniel Quinlan. It's been a great pleasure to work with Daniel, whose good-natured professionalism makes him an ideal editor. We are also grateful for the calm and efficient assistance of Emily Johnston, who headed up the production phase of this volume. Three anonymous reviewers gave careful and detailed attention to each of the individual contributions as well as to the volume as a whole. We thank them for their enormous and valuable effort. We would also like to take this opportunity to thank each of our authors for their diligence in responding to reviewer comments and for their timely submission of chapter revisions.

This book has been published with the help of a grant from the Canadian Federation for the Humanities and Social Sciences, through the Awards to Scholarly Publications Program, using funds provided by the Social Sciences and Humanities Research Council of Canada. We are very grateful for this support. Many thanks as well to Berkeley Fleming, Vice President and Provost at Mount Allison University, and the Department of Political Science at Simon Fraser University. We also thank Tsuneko Kokubo for allowing us to use Tree February (2009) as our cover image, which we think beautifully expresses the nuances of connectivity.

A special thanks to our partners, Steven Dodge and Stephen Law, and to our families for their unstinting support and encouragement.

Finally, we wish to express our gratitude to Iris Marion Young for her contributions to political theory and to our continuing intellectual development. We dedicate this book to her memory.

POLITICAL RESPONSIBILITY REFOCUSED

Thinking Justice after Iris Marion Young

1 Political Responsibility Refocused

LORALEA MICHAELIS AND GENEVIEVE
FUJI JOHNSON

Inspired by the last few published writings of Iris Marion Young, this collection of essays explores the conceptual foundations and practical implications of contemporary understandings of political responsibility that challenge the spatial and temporal boundaries of more traditional theories. As Young highlighted towards the end of her life, we live in an age in which we have become acutely aware of our interconnectivity, our vulnerability to chance, and the potentially limitless reach of our actions. This heightened understanding of the global contexts of politics, culture, economics, and the environment, in which even the most apparently local actions can have far-reaching consequences, has led to a shift in perspectives in popular as well as scholarly discussions of moral and political responsibility: individuals *and* societies and states have responsibilities to those living beyond the borders of their nations. The temporal limits of traditional theories of responsibility have become as flexible as the spatial. Publicly articulated claims to reparative justice by marginalized or oppressed groups and appeals to the interests and well-being of future generations by environmentalists have worked to extend our individual and collective responsibilities even further to include those who are no longer or not yet living.

The greater temporal and spatial reach of contemporary discussions of responsibility should be welcomed as an attempt to keep our moral and political aspirations in step with our deepening understanding of the world around us. This ambition is in itself a heartening confirmation of our potential for moral and political progress. But it raises a number of challenging theoretical and practical questions. It is not clear whether these far-reaching moral and political aspirations can be made theoretically coherent or whether even the most coherent theories of responsibility can be made practically intelligible. Exactly what theoretical support can be provided for these expanded responsibilities? Can these responsibilities be discharged in meaningful ways? Are there practices, policies, and institutions that could address these responsibilities?

The chapters in this volume offer critical assessments and elaborations of the temporal and spatial expansion that is occurring in contemporary discussions of political responsibility. Although there is considerable variation among the essays in their approach as well as in their overall judgment of the possibilities and limitations of this expansion, each takes as its point of departure the "social connection model" of political responsibility developed in rough outline by Young in her last works.[1] In this introduction, we set the broader context for this common focus on Young's model and mark out in more general terms the conceptual terrain upon which theories of political responsibility arise. The challenge for all of the political theorists who are contributors to this volume consists not only in coming to terms with the potentially limitless reach of our responsibilities but also in exploring the ways in which these responsibilities can be regarded as having a political and collective rather than simply moral and individual character. Young's social connection model is promising on both counts, in bounding the extent of our responsibilities without undermining the ground for their extension beyond what is contemplated in traditional theories and in clarifying and distinguishing their specific character as collective political responsibilities. On both counts, we offer this collection of essays under the title *Political Responsibility Refocused*.

Theories of political responsibility arise in the tradition of western political thought and in contemporary discussions of politics and public policy whenever questions of agency, accountability, and the consequences of action or inaction come into view. Although theories of political responsibility have often been developed alongside theories of political obligation and may well be little more than extensions of them, the one can be distinguished from the other insofar as the ascription of responsibility presumes a degree of agency and control over oneself and one's circumstances (i.e., a capacity to affect the course of events) that is not necessarily presumed in a theory of political obligation.[2] To raise the question of political responsibility in the context of a theory of political obligation is to raise particular questions about the capacities and circumstances that give us standing as moral and political agents from whom it is reasonable and just to expect certain kinds of actions: *to be responsible*, quite literally, is *to be able to respond* in morally and politically appropriate ways.

To raise questions about political responsibility is to ask not simply whether and how we should act but also whether and in what way we are capable of acting. It is to ask not simply whether our actions are consistent with our obligations but also whether our actions (or inactions) are deserving of praise or blame in light of the range of possibilities available to us. For this reason, as Young and others have noted, questions of political responsibility lend themselves to answers considerably more diffuse and indeterminate than the question of political obligation.[3] Our capacities and circumstances and thus our political responsibilities are subject to change in a way that our political obligations are not. It is also for this reason that the ascription of responsibility involves the exercise of practical judgment and relies upon a knowledge of contextual particulars – of specific capacities, circumstances, causal connections, and social relationships – more centrally than theories concerned with the ascription of obligation.[4]

Questions of political responsibility have been traditionally distinguished from questions of moral and legal responsibility in terms of an opposition between collective and individual agency: whereas individuals (and corporations, which are generally ascribed the status of individuals) alone can have moral and legal responsibilities, political responsibilities accrue to the political community as a whole.[5] We are morally responsible for our individual actions. Where our actions cause harm, we may appropriately be blamed or be found guilty. But responsibility for the actions of the political community has been more challenging to conceptualize.

In the liberal tradition, for which action is generally only the action of particular individuals, the responsibility of the group is often nothing more than the aggregate responsibility of its individual members: collective responsibility tends to reduce to individual responsibility. If there are no collective actions strictly speaking, then political responsibility is nothing more than the responsibility of particular individual citizens who have acted on behalf of the whole. Those citizens who have not acted per se cannot be held responsible. Concepts of group solidarity and shared benefit have been used to build stronger links between the responsibility of those members of the group who have acted and those who have not. For example, those citizens of developed countries who benefit from the exploitation of developing countries are responsible for this exploitation even though they have not directly participated in it. However, even here, the moral and legal framework of individual liability and guilt remains intact. Even here, political responsibility remains the responsibility of individual citizens who are first and foremost nothing more than individuals. Assigning and taking responsibility in these cases involves more clearly differentiating oneself as an individual agent rather than an anonymous and passive member of a group. This is the peculiar individualizing power for which, as Hannah Arendt noted, processes of assigning moral and legal liability (in public debates or in courtroom trials, for example) are justly celebrated. In such cases, the individual is drawn forward into the public view, drawn from the fabric of daily habits and relationships and group memberships in which his or her action was embedded and also, one might say, obscured as an action having moral significance. Criminal trials and war crimes tribunals charged with determining the guilt or innocence of particular individuals restore to them the autonomy that they would otherwise forfeit as cogs in a machine or hapless victims of circumstance or upbringing. The question that remains is whether or not political responsibility be conceptualized as something more than an extension of individual responsibility.

Arendt's development of the concept of political responsibility in her 1968 essay, "Collective Responsibility," takes particular issue with the tendency to collapse political responsibility into moral and legal responsibility. She finds this collapse indicative of the liberal inability to conceive of the political community as anything other than a voluntary association that can be as easily dissolved as a business partnership. For Arendt, political responsibility is the responsibility of a nonvoluntary association which is composed of individuals but which also exists independently of them. Although individuals can volunteer to become members of one community rather than another, they cannot choose, at least not plausibly – not without departing the human condition altogether – whether to become members at all. This nonvoluntary element gives the political association a different cast from more strictly voluntary associations such as business partnerships, which individuals *could* plausibly elect not to form at all. The political association of which we are necessarily a part has its own agency, a life of its own; as part of this association, we have responsibilities for what it does in our name. Whether "a whole community takes it upon itself to be responsible for whatever one of its members has done, or whether a community is being held responsible for what has been done in its name"[6] – this, for Arendt, is political responsibility.

Legal and moral conceptions of responsibility, Arendt says, "always relate to the person and what the person has done."[7] Questions of legal and moral responsibility are always tied up with questions of individual agency and raise the spectre of individual guilt. In contrast, Arendt grounds a conception of political responsibility on the integrity of the body politic as an actor in its own right. This body is authorized to act on behalf of its members and to bind those members on whose behalf it acts. It is also authorized to bind those who will act on its behalf in the future. We assume political responsibilities as a consequence of our membership in this association, which no one's voluntary act can dissolve, at least not without exchanging one's membership in an association for membership in another. Those who have no political responsibilities have no political membership whatsoever. Arendt was mindful of the objections with which this conception of political responsibility would meet, especially in the modern age in which a strong sense of the political collectivity is imperilled and a belief in the primacy of the individual is prevalent. The individualism that is the hallmark of liberal moral and political philosophy does address questions of collective and political responsibility but only, as Arendt highlights, by obscuring the inescapable sociability of the human situation. As she writes, this

> vicarious responsibility for things we have not done, this taking upon ourselves the consequences for things we are entirely innocent of, is the price we pay for the fact that we live our lives not by ourselves but among our fellow men, and that the faculty of action, which, after all, is the political faculty par excellence, can be actualized only in one of the many and manifold forms of human community.[8]

We, as a citizen body, have pressing political responsibilities that are not reducible to our individual moral and legal responsibilities.

The contemporary literature on political responsibility frequently applauds Arendt's project for moving beyond the individualism of conceptions of responsibility that do not take sufficient account of the political and social. But recourse to Arendt is by no means entire or seamless, in part because of the peculiar nature of problems prompting contemporary theorists of responsibility. Arendt's concern with questions of political responsibility was shaped by the experience of Nazism and the Nuremburg trials as well as early attempts, notably in the civil rights movement, to account for the responsibilities of putative "bystanders" to come to the aid of those who are suffering injustice or in peril of suffering injustice. Contemporary theorists of responsibility are motivated by a heightened consciousness of injustices that are more global and intergenerational in scope. Given this wider scope, the particular concept of the body politic which is central to Arendt's conception of political responsibility can have only limited application.

At the same time, theorists such as Young have taken advantage of the fluidity of Arendt's concept of the political to develop an account of political responsibility that extends beyond the borders of the nation state but that does not fall prey to what some have identified as the psychological as well as conceptual limitations of a theory of responsibility in which everybody is responsible for everybody and everything, everywhere.[9] This is the difficulty with which any theory of global or intergenerational justice must contend: once we know of the existence of injustice beyond our borders, such as piecemeal labour in extremely poor working conditions in sweatshops, and once we understand that future generations will have to live with the consequences of many of our decisions, such as those related to environmental degradation and climate change, how is it possible, if at all, to bound our seemingly boundless obligations? Young's particular attempt to find a way through this sort of difficulty was framed by the immediately pressing question of the developed world's responsibility for sweatshops in the developing world. While there is no shortage of theoretical support to be found among the various approaches within the contemporary literature for the position that sweatshops are wrong, there is a real scarcity of theoretical explorations of the question of whether and how this position should be acted upon, without, at least, leaving us helplessly burdened with responsibilities that are impossible to discharge. Herein lies the promise of Young's "social connection" model of political responsibility.

According to this model, we have obligations of justice to those beyond our borders. But we have these responsibilities only to the degree that we participate in social structures and processes that connect us to them. Young's social connection model of political responsibility offers a compelling redefinition of the body politic as having its foundation not in shared political institutions but in shared social and economic systems of interaction in which people mutually affect one another and for which shared political institutions become necessary "in order that people may collectively regulate those interactions in ways they judge most just."[10] It is these shared social connections that *call for* the creation of shared political institutions, as a means of discharging the responsibilities that we have incurred as a result of our social connections.

Young's social connection model departs from more traditional thinking on political responsibility not only in its redefinition of the body politic but also in its clarification of the temporal priorities of political responsibility as distinct from moral and legal responsibility. Moreover, Young's understandings of these forms of responsibility differ somewhat from Arendt's. Young argues that thinking about responsibility has been dominated by juridical considerations of liability and blame for past harms and necessarily focuses on harms and injustices for which there are identifiable perpetrators. Conversely, political responsibility is more forward-looking and imposes obligations of redress on those who might not necessarily have been responsible (in a causal sense) for the harm: it seeks, as she says, "not to reckon debts" but "to bring about results, and thus depends on the actions of everyone who is in a position to contribute to the results."[11] In this way, Young's argument recalls Arendt's suggestive characterization of political responsibility as a responsibility *for things we have not done* but a responsibility that we nonetheless bear as a consequence of our membership in a political association that no voluntary act can dissolve.[12] For Young, however, it is our participation in social processes rather than citizenship that confers this responsibility: we become responsible for redressing harms that we may not have caused directly but to which we contribute through our participation in social processes that systematically produce these harms. Again, for Young, political responsibility is forward- rather than backward-looking in the sense that the redress of harms requires positive action undertaken with a view to the future. Political responsibility also involves making changes in our norms, practices, and institutions so that they minimize inequalities and injustices for distant people.

Young's work on the social connection model of political responsibility builds upon her earlier influential work on the concept of structural injustice; this influence is evident in many of the essays collected in this volume. For Young, theories of justice traditionally focus on distributive issues. Even where more complex concepts such as domination or oppression are deployed, as they are in radical theories of justice that aim to go beyond the liberal preoccupation with rights and resources, the focus remains on the issue of distribution: power is included among the many goods that are unequally distributed, an instrument to be wielded by the few who have it over the many who do not. Young argued that this focus on distribution is unable to address forms of injustice that may have a distributive dimension but exist even under cover of equal distribution. Such is the case, for example, with racism, sexism, and homophobia, which persist long after legal and distributive victories. To give a name to these forms of injustice, and to clarify concepts of domination and oppression having long-standing currency among radical activists, Young introduced the concept of structural injustice: domination and oppression are forms of structural injustice that have their source not in the actions of a ruling group but in the often subtle constraints "embedded in unquestioned norms, habits, and symbols, in the assumptions underlying institutional rules and the collective consequences of following those rules."[13] Although Young's early work on structural injustice was a major breakthrough in naming and analysing the scope of the problem, it did not provide much guidance on the question of its remedy. Such a question is complicated by the fact that structural injustices have their source in the systemic accretion of norms and practices rather than the discrete actions of particular individuals. But the fact that there is no one at fault for such injustices does not mean that no one is responsible for their redress. It is this insight that grounds the analysis of social relations and networks that is called for by the social connection model of political responsibility on which Young was working at the time of her death. Insofar as it is aimed directly at the question of how to conceptualize the responsibility for the redress of harms for which, strictly speaking, there is no one to blame, this model extends and completes Young's early analysis of structural injustice.

Young's social connection model holds out the promise of a more definite, more concrete account of our responsibility for global justice than would seem to be the case in other cosmopolitan or humanitarian models: even though we have responsibilities for those who live beyond our borders we are not necessarily responsible for everyone and everything everywhere. But it is not clear in the end how well this promise is realized in the social connection model. If the borders of the political community are too rigid to accommodate the obligations that we have to other human beings regardless of their citizenship, the borders of the social seem far too lax to bound these obligations, at least in such a way as to make it possible to imagine their meaningful discharge.

Arendt's concept of political responsibility – as a responsibility for things that have been done in the name of the political community of which we are members – is anchored firmly in the shared experience of citizenship. Our obligations to others, even to those beyond the borders of our political community, have their foundation in our shared experience of membership in that community. The political responsibilities that we incur on Arendt's model are collective rather than individual responsibilities and can be meaningfully discharged only by the collectivity – namely, by those who act on its behalf. But the social connection model, anchored in social connections and social systems of which there is not necessarily any shared common understanding, would seem to lack this collective experiential foundation.

The political responsibilities that Young's social connection model confers would seem to be primarily the responsibilities of individuals who have developed a heightened awareness of the many systems of structural injustice and of their own location within those systems. To be sure, the individuals with whom Young is concerned are thoroughly embedded in social relations. They assume their responsibility for overcoming systems of structural injustice, as beneficiaries or as victims, as members of social groups first and foremost. The social connection model of political responsibility is a call to collective action issued to these social groups. To this extent, Young's social connection model avoids the diminution of political responsibility to the project of individual self-perfection that we might expect (in an Arendtian spirit) to follow from the greater priority that it gives to the social community. Young does not make this as clear as she might have, however. In the absence of vibrant transnational social movements to give expression and organization to the transnational aspirations of justice-seeking social groups – to give body to a common experience of transnational political responsibility – the social connection model risks precisely this diminution. Indeed, a number of issues and questions remain unclear or unaddressed. After all, this model was in its early stages at the time of Young's death in 2006. As Martha Nussbaum notes in her foreword to Young's posthumously published *Responsibility for Justice*,[14] it falls to us to continue the work of development and clarification.

In our volume, the first three chapters bring into focus the conceptual possibilities as well as limitations of the social connection model for thinking about issues of justice that transcend relations between citizens. Young's social connection model of political responsibility is not confined to issues of global justice, but it is in the field of global justice studies that it has been most deeply mined. It is in reference to the question of the responsibilities of consumers of manufactured goods produced through sweatshop industries located in other countries that Young herself applied the social connection model of responsibility.

Part of the reason, as Margaret Moore emphasizes in Chapter 2, "Global Justice and the Connection Theory of Responsibility," is that theories of global justice must contend with a reality in which "there are few agents and institutions that have been assigned or have taken responsibility for addressing global injustices." If we have duties that are global in scope, then how are we to discharge these duties? How do we act in the absence of the mediating and remedial institutions on which we rely when we seek remedies for harms that occur within our own borders and between fellow citizens? These questions are complicated by the fact that the injustices often cited in the global justice literature involve harms that do not necessarily involve a single or clearly identifiable agent. Examples are gross economic exploitation (child and piecemeal labour), deprivation caused by a succession of unrelated actors and actions (destitute poverty), and finally collective harms arising from uncoordinated individual actions compounded over time (climate change and pollution).

As Moore argues in her chapter, ordinary language understandings of justice and responsibility are insufficient to account for the complexity of these harms. The traditional, or phenomenological, account of responsibility, which focuses on individual agency and liability for specific harms, has clear advantages over utilitarian accounts that make individuals responsible for correcting even those harms that they have not caused directly on the grounds that it is more beneficial to correct harms than not. Agency must remain the anchoring concept in a theory of responsibility, Moore argues, if we are to avoid the pitfall of assigning responsibilities that could never be discharged adequately, and if we are to retain the ability to distinguish degrees of responsibility to reflect different degrees of agency. But the traditional approach runs into difficulties with assigning responsibilities for collective harms for which there is no clear agent. More particularly, it cannot address the gap in theories of global justice when it comes to assigning responsibility for creating the global institutions through which alone harms that are global in scope could be remedied. This is where Young's social connection model of responsibility marks a real advance over the traditional, in Moore's view. The responsibility to create institutions aimed correcting global harms is assigned to those who are embedded in the relational networks that create, perpetuate, or receive benefits from the injustice or harm. However, Moore suggests that Young's model of responsibility bears greater affinities to the traditional than Young herself acknowledges. The web of social connection that is foregrounded in Young's theory of responsibility does not so much eclipse the phenomenological focus on agency and liability as give it a stronger foundation. Indeed, the phenomenological approach is helpful in clarifying and strengthening Young's model where it seems to give insufficient attention, at least on the surface, to questions of agency, intention, and choice. The greatest advance of the social connection model of responsibility over the traditional, Moore concludes, is its greater applicability to collective harms such as climate change, where the agency involved is not the agency of any one individual but the genuinely shared agency that comes into view as the combined effects of individual actions. The reconstruction of this shared agency yields the idea of shared responsibility with which Young's social connection model is primarily concerned.

In Chapter 3, "Power and Responsibility," J.L. Schiff, like Moore, is interested in the implications of Young's social connection model for thinking about responsibility for collective harms such as climate change and financial crises. She also identifies points of overlap between Young's model and the more traditional model of responsibility. However, she finds in this overlap a shortcoming rather than a strength. Schiff argues that Young's social connection model has in common with the liability model a commodified conception of power as a resource to be used, whereby those who have the most power in this sense are deemed to be the most responsible. Moore also draws attention to this implication of Young's argument. Even as the social connection model of responsibility casts a wider net to include not only those who directly cause structural injustice (as in the liability model) but also those who benefit from or indirectly contribute to it, it still limits shared responsibility to those who are able to respond. For example, the mother on welfare who takes advantage of the low cost of clothes produced through sweatshop labour is not understood as responsible for its redress, as are more privileged consumers who have more choice concerning where to shop and how much to pay for clothes. But where Moore is assured that Young's social connection model of responsibility is still able to recognize the importance of agency in the determination of responsibility, Schiff is concerned that Young's model gives insufficient recognition to the responsibility of individuals suffering from structural injustice. They would seem to have no political responsibilities whatsoever. They would seem to be excluded, paradoxically, from the community of those who share responsibility for the redress of the structural injustices from which they benefit or to which they indirectly contribute.

In order to realize the conceptual advance that Young's social connection model makes over the liability model, Schiff argues for a more nuanced understanding of the relationship between power and responsibility. She draws on Arendt, Foucault, and Bourdieu to explore an account of power that reflects not only its commodified and instrumental aspect as a resource for achieving particular ends but also its constitutive, disciplinary, and symbolic aspects as a capacity that emerges, Schiff writes, only "when human beings are together and act in concert." Power in this sense is not something that we *have* or *use* but something that we *create* in the relationships that we establish with each other. This more thoroughly relational conception of power, she argues, is the appropriate conceptual analogue to Young's relational conception of responsibility: shared responsibility consists in coming together to develop the capacities to respond to structural injustice that would otherwise remain undeveloped. Schiff's interpretation of Young's conception of shared responsibility as the enabling of collective action has particular bearing on the redress of harms and injustices that are global in scope and for which, in consequence, there are few pre-existing institutions or organizations. For Schiff as for Moore, then, the conceptual power of Young's social connection model resides in its refocusing of political responsibility as a forward-looking responsibility to create nothing less than a transnational political community. Although transnational it is not all-encompassing, as in traditional cosmopolitanism. Its borders are set by the social connections that have been mapped by its own members.

In Chapter 4, "Autonomous Development and Global Empowerment," Nancy Bertoldi provides a substantive example of this transnational mapping, taking the foundational ideas behind Young's social connection model of responsibility as the inspiration for a feminist agenda of global empowerment. Bertoldi approaches Young's latest work on political responsibility as the culmination of a longer-term theoretical project beginning with her early contributions to feminist theory. Bertoldi draws from Young's project a broad "paradigm of autonomous development" that has four conceptual dimensions: a relational conception of agency, a critique of domination and oppression in social relations, an analysis of structural injustice, and a model of political responsibility grounded in social connection. In her elaboration of each of these dimensions of Young's project, Bertoldi details the challenge that it poses to traditional concepts and frameworks for thinking about gender equality and global politics and suggests directions for future research and activism. Bertoldi's analysis brings Young's account of political responsibility more clearly into the field of feminist theory in which she made her original contributions, not only clarifying its implications for the feminist project of empowerment for women but also suggesting the framework for a comprehensive theory of democratic citizenship and global justice.

In the next two chapters, the emphasis shifts from the spatial to the temporal implications of recent theories of political responsibility. In Chapter 5, "Political Responsibility for Decolonization in Canada," Melissa Williams explores the different models of political responsibility to which we may turn for guidance in thinking about the question of who is responsible for the project of decolonization in Canada and beyond. Prompted by Canadian prime minister Stephen Harper's apology to Indigenous peoples for the past injustice of the residential school policy which was pursued as part of a broader colonial policy of assimilation in Canada since the 1840s, Williams suggests that acts of taking responsibility in public apologies need to be carefully assessed in light of the capacity to discharge the reparative responsibilities that such apologies presume but cannot necessarily deliver. Part of the difficulty, she argues, is that there is more than one way of taking responsibility, each varying in the degree and scope of the agency that it requires as well as the specific nature of the duties that it ordains. Distinguishing between fiduciary, liability, social contract, and social connection models of responsibility, Williams's analysis provides a compelling overview of the conceptual terrain upon which theories of political responsibility can be developed and evaluated. Although there are significant points of conflict between the different models – in particular, between the inequality presumed by the fiduciary model and the equality presumed by the social contract model – there are also important areas of complementarity and overlap, so that, as Williams argues, no one model is adequate on its own. Williams's argument in favour of a hybrid model of political responsibility gives particular priority to the social connection model developed by Young on account of its comprehensiveness as a model of political responsibility that goes well beyond the liability model in engaging the entire citizen body in a duty of solidarity with

Indigenous peoples. Here, recalling Arendt, Young prompts the revival of a line of thinking about political responsibility in which we are responsible for harms for which we cannot be blamed but which we are required to attempt to repair.

In Chapter 6, "Social Connections and Our Political Responsibilities to Future Generations," Genevieve Fuji Johnson explores the conceptual possibilities of Young's social connection model for thinking about our responsibilities to future generations. The literature on intergenerational justice offers two main approaches: the utilitarian, according to which we in the present are responsible for maximizing the happiness of future generations, and the deontological, according to which we are responsible to assure that future generations do not inherit a narrower range of rights, choices, and opportunities than we currently enjoy. Although each approach provides compelling theoretical grounds for the intuition that future generations should be taken into account when we in the present make decisions that could potentially affect them, neither is able to answer adequately the question of whether and how we would be able to discharge this responsibility. In both cases, our responsibilities to future generations appear to be so abstract and so general as to be unmanageable and, indeed, not dischargeable. Exactly how can we maximize the welfare of future generations in the absence of complete information regarding the size of the population (always a consideration in utilitarian calculations) and future conceptions of pleasures and pains that could be very different from our own? And exactly how can equal moral standing and equal rights be granted to non-existent persons? How could the rights claims of these non-existent persons be adjudicated? What kind of remedy could be provided for their violation? Johnson offers Young's social connection model as an alternative way of thinking about our responsibilities to future generations that avoids the pitfalls of both the utilitarian and deontological models. Johnson's discussion of Young draws temporal implications from the expansive spatial reach of her social connection model while at the same time highlighting the ways in which this model can be used to circumscribe the nature and extent of our responsibilities to future generations. In particular, Johnson uses Young's model to anchor these responsibilities in the network of social relations and structures that we inherit from previous generations and hand down to those that follow after. Specific responsibilities to future generations would arise within this network, framed by policy-specific processes and issues, and limited to the consideration of consequences that can be reasonably foreseen. As Johnson emphasizes, Young's social connection model provides a more circumscribed account of the scope and reach of our responsibilities to future generations than the utilitarian and deontological models.

As all of the chapters in this volume attest, theories of political responsibility share in common an attempt to forge a stronger connection between obligation and action. They are occupied with the question of not just what we are obliged to do but also whether and how we can discharge our obligations. This connection between obligation and action is most explicitly theorized in the final two contributions by Tanja Pritzlaff and Adrian Neer. In Chapter 7, "Political Practices as Performances of Political Responsibility," Pritzlaff explores the conceptual possibilities of Young's social connection model of responsibility through the lens of practice theory. Practice theory is concerned with social practices as normative "performances" that can embody and preserve as well as challenge the institutions and structures of a society. Drawing a distinction between implicit and explicit norms, practice theorists argue that the normative dimension of practices consists not just in rule following but also in the implicit norms that are actualized in our interactions with each other. This distinction between implicit and explicit norms is most sharply evident in the possibility of their coming into conflict – for example, in the case of hypocrisy, in which an individual professes a commitment to a principle of justice that is contradicted by the way in which he or she actually behaves. Practice theory aims to develop a systematic theory of the implicit normativity of practices to which this common-sense example of the hypocrite obliquely refers. Although Young does not invoke the distinction between implicit and explicit norms, Pritzlaff suggests that her social connection model of political responsibility can be understood in these terms. Young's social connection model of political responsibility sets aside as incomplete the traditional focus on past-oriented questions of liability and guilt and foregrounds instead the future-oriented question of how we can act upon our commitment to eliminate the structural injustices to which we are linked. In so doing it prompts a critical review of the norms that are embedded in our habitual and unreflected practices and interactions – indeed, to see, perhaps for the first time, our practices as normatively charged interactions with unseen others – and also a consideration of the ways in which we might act upon this normatively charged environment so as to transform it. What Young's social connection model of responsibility offers, as Pritzlaff aptly writes, is an idea of "political action that performs responsibility rather than asks for it." By bringing into clearer focus the implicit normativity of political action, the social connection model of political responsibility, seen through the lens of practice theory, does not so much replace the traditional focus of theories of justice on explicit rules and principles as ground them more securely.

In Chapter 8, "Institutional Responsibility and Belonging in Political Community," Neer considers the stronger connection that theories of political responsibility aspire to forge between obligation and action in light of the questions about institutional realization that such theories raise but to some extent leave unanswered. By focusing on the question of institutionalization, Neer also highlights the importance of the collectivity to theories of political responsibility such as Young's in which, strictly speaking, no one individual could plausibly be fully responsible. Quoting from Young, Neer writes: "'Obligations of social justice are not primarily owed by individuals to individuals. Instead, they concern primarily the organization of institutions.'" But just how adequately, Neer asks, do theories of political responsibility that are transnational in scope conceptualize the particular institutional settings for upholding and acting upon these collective responsibilities? For theorists such as Young, the institutions of the nation state are no longer adequate to address the complex webs of interdependence by which individuals and collectivities are linked across state boundaries. This interdependence creates principles of justice that state-centred theories of justice do not fully recognize. However, as Neer argues, these "post-Westphalian" theories of justice have only begun to address the question of the institutional arrangements – notably the relationship between state and nonstate actors – that would be required to implement the transnational principles to which they are committed. Neer is particularly critical of the inattention to the continuing importance of the state as having the advantage of territoriality and sovereignty over nonstate actors in discharging political responsibilities. But he does not recommend a return to a state-centred theory of political responsibility. Any answer to the question of how to allocate institutional political responsibility in a globalized environment must take account of the fact that the state is one institution among many and, following Young, that the institutions that are being created to match webs of interdependence also must be made accountable to the political communities whose interests and identities they express.

All of the chapters in this volume undertake to provide clarification, extension, and critical assessment of recent thinking on political responsibility that, with Young, address our growing sense that we are responsible for injustices and harms that occur beyond our borders and that are not necessarily the result of actions undertaken directly by us or in our name. Political responsibility is fundamentally linked to an ever-expanding sociability that generates principles of justice, which are uncertain in scope and for which our current conceptual vocabulary and political institutions are inadequate or incomplete. To what extent and in what way these far reaching responsibilities are conceptualized as specifically *political* responsibilities not easily reducible to the moral and legal responsibilities of individuals vary in the chapters collected here. There is also considerable variation in how far and in what way the vocabulary of political responsibility is distinguished from the vocabulary of political obligation. These variations reflect not only the different theoretical traditions from which the authors approach the question of political responsibility but also, and more importantly, the novelty of the field of questions with which the authors are contending. It is to the cultivation of this field that our volume is devoted.

NOTES

1 Iris Marion Young, "Responsibility and Global Labor Justice," *Journal of Political Philosophy* 12 (2004): 365–88, and Young, "Responsibility and Global Justice: A Social Connection Model," *Social Philosophy and Policy* 23 (2006): 102–30.

2 We offer this distinction between responsibility and obligation as an opening position in a more complex discussion, mindful of the fact that the contributors to this volume may use these terms interchangeably or may uphold a different understanding of the distinction itself.

3 Iris Marion Young, "Responsibility, Social Connection, and Global Labour Justice," in *Global Challenges: War, Self-determination and Responsibility for Justice* (Cambridge: Polity, 2007), 182. Here, Young is following Joel Feinberg's distinction between an ethic of obligation or duty on the one hand and, on the other, an ethic of responsibility. See Joel Feinberg, "Duties, Rights, and Claims," in *Rights, Justice and the Bounds of Liberty*, ed. Feinberg (Princeton, NJ: Princeton University Press, 1980), 135–40.

4 For example, Marion Smiley, in *Moral Responsibility and the Boundaries of Community* (Chicago: University of Chicago Press, 1992), places particular

emphasis on ascriptions of responsibility as judgments of blameworthiness that vary according to the social and political perspective of the one making the judgment rather than factual determinations of causal agency.

5 There is an extensive philosophical literature on responsibility which is primarily concerned with the individual from a moral and legal perspective, governed by questions of free will, liability, intent, causation, and criminality. See, for example, Laura Waddell Ekstrom, ed., *Agency and Responsibility: Essays on the Metaphysics of Freedom* (Boulder, CO: Westview, 2001), and R.G. Frey and Christopher W. Morris, eds., *Liability and Responsibility: Essays in Law and Morals* (Cambridge: Cambridge University Press, 2008). Because the moral and legal literatures on responsibility take the individual person as the bearer of responsibility, the concept of political responsibility is raised in this literature only by way of the (necessarily controversial, for this approach) concept of collective or group responsibility – for instance, in Larry May and Stacey Joffman, *Collective Responsibility: Five Decades of Debate in Theoretical and Applied Ethics* (Lanham, MD: Rowman Littlefield, 1992). Even where the theme of political responsibility is addressed directly, as in Ian MacLean, Alan Montefiore, and Peter Winch, eds., *The Political Responsibility of Intellectuals* (Cambridge: Cambridge University Press, 1991), it is considered primarily in moral/individual terms, in this case, with specific reference to the functions and duties of intellectuals.

6 Hannah Arendt, "Collective Responsibility," in *Responsibility and Judgement*, ed. Jerome Kohn (New York: Schocken Books, 2003), 148.

7 Ibid.

8 Ibid., 158.

9 See Iris Marion Young's engagement with Arendt in "Responsibility and Global Labor Justice," *Journal of Political Philosophy* 12, no. 4 (2004): 275–7. For the challenge to which Young is responding, see Samuel Scheffler, "Individual Responsibility in a Global Age," in *Boundaries and Allegiances: Problems of Responsibility and Justice in Liberal Thought* (Oxford: Oxford University Press, 2001), 39.

10 Young, "Responsibility and Global Labor Justice," 376.

11 Ibid., 379.

12 Arendt, "Collective Responsibility," 149.

13 Iris Marion Young, *Justice and the Politics of Difference* (Princeton, NJ: Princeton University Press, 1990), 41.

14 Martha C. Nussbaum, "Foreword," in Iris Marion Young, *Responsibility for Justice* (Oxford: Oxford University Press, 2011), xxv.

2 Global Justice and the Connection Theory of Responsibility

MARGARET MOORE[1]

This chapter focuses on the concept of responsibility as it has figured in scholarly debates in global justice. The issue of responsibility is central in the global justice literature in part because there are few agents and institutions that have been assigned or have taken responsibility for addressing global injustices. Many duties that we might think of as taking hold at the global level (e.g., duties to alleviate severe poverty, help the sick, protect human rights, and create more fair institutions) are imperfect in the sense that while everyone may be said to have them, no one in particular can be identified as responsible to act on them. Moreover, at the global level, there are exceedingly complex interrelationships among a number of agents making it difficult to pinpoint exact "backward-looking" responsibility for a state of affairs that is unjust. This challenges our ordinary language understandings of both responsibility and justice in ways that will be elaborated ahead.

Some of the most innovative academic writing on responsibility has emerged in response to issues in the global justice debate. Among them is Iris Marion Young's work on the "shared connection" model.[2] In this chapter, I examine the coherence, plausibility, and usefulness of this model and its relationship to "inter-actionist" and luck egalitarian accounts of global justice.[3] In the first part, I will examine the traditional account of responsibility, in which responsibility is tied to our agency. This is the so-called traditional or agency account of responsibility, which is described by Samuel Scheffler.[4] I will then outline three major problems of global justice and injustice and the extent to which they are addressed in the traditional account of responsibility. In the second part, I situate Young's account within cosmopolitan theories of global justice – of either the luck egalitarian or interactionist variety. Young's theory, I argue, is a version of interactionism. In the third part, I will outline Young's shared connection model, which is intended to improve on the traditional account and is specifically addressed to the global order. In the fourth part, I will assess Young's theory both in terms of its plausibility as a theory of responsibility and its usefulness for dealing with major issues of global justice and injustice. I will argue that her theory is an improvement over the traditional account, associated with standard types of liberal theory, and outlined persuasively by Scheffler, especially in its treatment of collective harms, but that it faces similar difficulties (unconnected to the account of responsibility) in dealing with exploitation. Young's model offers a plausible account of dealing with harms caused by multiple agents but only insofar as it relies on the idea of agency, which is at the heart of the traditional account of responsibility.

Part One: The Traditional Account of Responsibility and Global Justice Problems

In this section, I set out the traditional, or phenomenological, view of moral responsibility, which is the dominant view, mainly drawing on Scheffler's work, to establish a baseline from which to compare Young's innovative connection theory of responsibility.

There are three central tenets of the traditional view of moral responsibility: (1) an emphasis on individualism, whereby people are the primary bearers of responsibility; (2) a distinction between positive and negative duties, whereby people believe it is worse to harm directly than either harm indirectly or fail to prevent harm; and (3) the importance of special obligations – that is, the importance of family, friends, and colleagues. This conception seems "natural" to us because it fits our conception of ourselves as agents, primarily in giving priority to action over omission, to near over remote outcomes, and to individual over group behaviour.[5] This conception is a fairly traditional one, in that it is intended to match the limits of our agency. It is intended to match how we reason about people to whom we are attached and the special duties to which these relationships give rise (e.g., relationships to friends and to family members). It also attempts to match our sense of our own efficacy in the world and the extent to which we can reasonably foresee the consequences of our own actions. This explains the requirement that the consequences should be a direct result of our individual actions.

This conception was developed in a more rigorous form in part through a critique of utilitarianism's account of responsibility, which was unduly demanding. Consider Peter Singer's utilitarian account of our global duties.[6] Singer argued from utilitarian premises for the principle that "if it is in our power to prevent something bad from happening, without thereby sacrificing something of comparable moral importance, we ought, morally, to do it."[7] He offered, as an example of the direct application of the foregoing principle, the following:

> If I am walking past a shallow pond and see a child drowning in it, I ought to wade in and pull the child out. This will mean getting my clothes muddy, while the death of the child would presumably be a very bad thing.[8]

Although this example is very compelling, critics have argued that it gains plausibility precisely because it is too simplistic. In the real world, there is not merely one child drowning in the pond but there are millions of them (metaphorically) and the said person would never get to work at all, as she would be busy pulling children out from dusk to dawn. The principle seems to require this, and critics have argued that it is too demanding, for it fails to leave room for the agent's own projects, aims, and life. Moreover, no attention is paid to how the child ended up in the pond in the first place. In particular, there is no attempt to track those who are responsible (in a backward-looking way) for this state of affairs (which might be a case of criminal negligence or of even actively pushing the child into the pond) in the account of responsibility. In short, the utilitarian account, which derives our duties from an impartial perspective, has been criticized as both too demanding and failing to match our conception of our own agency.[9] The traditional model of responsibility, by contrast, attempts to track the limits of our own (individual) agency, and this agent-centred account of responsibility is more modest than the utilitarian account that it developed in response to.

In addition, we often think that there is a moral difference between positive and negative duties. At the very least, we should refrain from harming other people or violating their rights no matter what the net benefit might be. This is more important, more linked to our agency, than simply failing to help others or failing to prevent harm perpetrated by others.[10] In part this is because it is difficult to foresee all the effects of our inaction, whereas the direct effects of our actions can usually be reasonably foreseen, and this is relevant to the question of our (moral) responsibility.

While the traditional account does accord better than the utilitarian account with our own sense of our agency, it is also problematic: it fails to hold anyone responsible for many of the central cases of global injustices. Consider three kinds of serious problems, often considered injustices, that arise at the global level: (1) exploitation (e.g., economic interaction with mutual but unfair benefit); (2) severe deprivation or harm caused by multiple actors (and in many cases where a person is in a severely deprived state, we can identify numerous people who were in a position to act differently and either contributed to or failed to help the person get out of the severely deprived state); and (3) collective harms resulting from multiple, uncoordinated similar actions, none of which on its own would be harmful (e.g., driving cars). In this chapter, I will discuss the inadequacy of the traditional account of responsibility in dealing with the second and third kinds of problems, and compare this to Young's connection theory account.

Exploitation

Most contributors to the literature on responsibility in global justice discuss exploitation as a serious problem.[11] This is one of the few areas of agreement between cosmopolitan and noncosmopolitan (or more statist) accounts. All contributors agree on some kind of non-exploitation principle. One difficulty with this is that it's difficult to identify an independent account of what counts as exploitation. Of course, Marxists have such an account, in which case exploitation necessarily occurs at the hands of the owners of the means of production, and in traditional Marxist theory workers are exploited if they produce surplus value.[12] Most people in the global justice debate, however, use exploitation as a kind of emotive word for an agreement or interaction that is profoundly unfair. On this understanding, exploitation is not an independent concept because it is derived from an account of fairness – both in the sense of a conception of fair starting points and an account of fair processes.[13] When these are lacking, we might say that the agreement was uncoerced but exploitative. In this context, the term "exploitative" means something like "severely unfair."

If this is our conception of exploitation – and I believe that most people mean something like this – then, while the principle of non-exploitation is somewhat problematic, the difficulties do not rest with the link between exploitation and the theory of responsibility. The problem with the discussion of exploitation is partly practical: we lack global institutions to ensure that bargains are not exploitative, and we lack mechanisms to adjudicate and punish those who are guilty of exploitative practices. It is also partly disagreement about what counts as exploitation. We do not want to rule out all unfair agreements because even unfair agreements can be mutually beneficial (indeed, why else would one agree?). If we don't rule out all unfair agreements, it is difficult to identify a point at which unfair agreements are unacceptable and count as exploitative.[14]

If we think of an agreement between X and Y as unfair – an agreement made from unfair or unequal initial positions, through a process that also is unfair, resulting in an unfair or inequitable distribution of benefits – then we can clearly identify the violation of a duty of justice (i.e., a duty not to exploit others). This is indeed how the duty is described in much of the philosophical writing on the subject. But most kinds of exploitation actually shade into another issue that frequently arises in the global justice literature, where the harm or deprivation is complexly related to a multiplicity of agents. This is especially true when there is a structural dimension to the unfairness, so that the unfair starting point or unfair process of agreement can be related to differential power relations.

Multiple Actors

This brings us to the second kind of problem confronted in the global justice literature, which will be dealt with at some length in the chapter. This is the problem that many states of deprivation or injustice are actually the result of multiple possible and potential actions by many agents. They do not fit the simple case of agent A interacting with agent B in an exploitative or harmful way. Consider, for example, the case of X, who is severely deprived. He is cold, homeless, and hungry. How did he get into this situation? A number of factors and agents may have contributed to this. His friend G may have encouraged his drinking and so led to his suffering from alcoholism. I may have fired him from his job. His partner, unhappy with his lack of employment and unproductive drinking, may have thrown him out of their shared house. He may have passed seven or eight people on the street, begging them for money for a hot lunch, or bus fare to get to a rehabilitation centre, and they refused him. All of these actions, some positive actions, some failures to act, but all of them seemingly legitimate, may have contributed to his situation. With few options left, he agrees to an exploitative but still beneficial agreement, which is at least better than living on the street. Many, many agents have contributed to this state of affairs, but according to the traditional account we cannot hold them *responsible*.

As noted earlier, the traditional account requires that responsibility can be ascribed only if the injustice is the *direct* result of an action (which rules out G's role in the foregoing case); the result of positive actions, rather than failure to act (which rules out the numerous people who failed to help); and a result that excludes the indirect effects of otherwise legitimate market actions or decisions in the personal realm.[15] In most cases of global poverty, the situation is dire and in need of remedy. But most of the causal levers are indirect, the result of inaction on the part of many people, or the result of unintended and unforeseen actions whose outcomes are at some distance from each agent. Commenting on the interconnectedness of many actions and decisions, Thomas Pogge writes,

> It is impossible to know which of our decisions have such effects on people in the poor countries, and what their effects are exactly. This is unknown because, as they reverberate around the globe, the effects of my economic decisions intermingle with the effects of billions of decisions made by others, and it is impossible to try to disentangle, even ex post, the impact of *my* decisions from this vast traffic by trying to figure out how things would have gone had I acted differently.[16]

Since this is so, Scheffler argues that deprivations in this sort of multiple agency case fail the test of responsibility-attribution. We cannot hold people responsible for consequences that they couldn't adequately foresee and didn't intend. We cannot hold people responsible for failure to act (indeed, if we did that, at what point does our responsibility end?). Such an extensive model of responsibility wouldn't match our sense of ourselves as agents. It would be extremely demanding, not only in terms of the extent of our duties. More seriously, it would be difficult to shape our lives according to our own choices and sense of ourselves as actors in the world. Scheffler notes that the more extensive view of responsibility is in danger of making "wildly excessive demands on the capacity of agents to amass information about the global impact of the different courses of action available to them."[17]

Collective Harms

A third difficulty for the traditional model of responsibility is that this model of responsibility-attribution cannot hold us responsible for collective harms. By "collective harms," I am referring to cases where actions are not harmful if done individually but are harmful if done by a threshold number of similarly acting people. This is indeed the paradigm case of human-induced global climate change, which the traditional theory, with its individualist focus and its emphasis on direct, rather than indirect, outcomes, cannot deal with adequately. The harm generated by carbon emissions is not directly, or solely, the result of individual action. Indeed, even if I drive a large SUV, which is far beyond what I need to get to work every day, the pollution generated by this in itself doesn't cause global warming. The carbons emitted by me do not cause any harm by themselves. The problem arises not because of my actions but because millions of people like me live a lifestyle that involves greenhouse gas emissions. It is our uncoordinated individual actions that together cause harm to the environment. On the traditional conception of responsibility, I cannot be blamed for harm when it is not my individual action by itself that caused harm, but rather the fact that this action occurred at the same time as millions of other, uncoordinated individual actions that collectively produced so much carbon pollution that they have a harmful impact on global climate change. Because the individual harm or effects caused by burning fossil fuels are negligible, the individual cannot be held accountable for this harm in a traditional sense.[18]

Further, the traditional conception of moral responsibility, which follows our conception of what we do and feel from the agent perspective, takes into account whether, from the agent's perspective, there are reasonable alternatives. The fact that we may not have many choices in the matter (e.g., there is little public transport, not everyone can live within walking distance to their work or places of school and leisure, and, indeed, the whole way of life is organized around the car) seems to reduce the moral responsibility that each individual bears for his or her action. After all, how can you be held responsible for your actions when there are few viable alternatives?

If my description of this traditional model of responsibility is accurate, it is seriously flawed in that it is unable to attribute responsibility for human-induced global warming. It cannot attribute praise or blame to individuals or provide a basis for remedying the situation (assuming there is a link between moral and remedial responsibility). Indeed, it is inadequate in dealing with all cases with a collective action problem structure (i.e., where many uncoordinated individual actions produce harm, but there is no harm in each individual making independent choices of a certain kind).

Part Two: Cosmopolitan Theories of Justice and Responsibility

In this section, I describe Young's social connection theory of responsibility, in contrast both to the traditional, agency-centred account of responsibility and noninteractionist accounts of justice and responsibility.

One of Young's principal aims is to theorize the responsibilities that moral agents have towards one another. She argues that obligations of justice arise by virtue of the social processes that connect them and that all people connected to these global social processes have responsibilities to work to remedy injustice.[19] In order to see the importance of this model and the role that it plays in debates on global justice, it is important to compare it with cosmopolitan, noninteractionist accounts of global justice and the implicit conception of responsibility.

Cosmopolitan accounts of global justice generally seek to justify the creation of better global institutions to deal more effectively with global problems. There are very good reasons for thinking that institutional change would be beneficial. Indeed, in many cases global problems can be dealt with effectively only at the institutional and not the individual level.[20] However, these accounts don't show that individuals have a responsibility to create institutions to regulate these serious moral problems.

I argue that an account of the creation of institutions to address global harms or to solve global problems should not be conceived of as simply assigned, and created through legitimate political processes, but should also be seen as derived from individual responsibilities. Only then could we have an account of how institutional assigned responsibility tracks our preinstitutional responsibility. We could then see new or better global institutions as the means by which we dispense our duties of justice, especially when we are confronted with a complex global problem such as global poverty or human-induced climate change (especially when, as in the latter case, the problem has important coordination features).

We have seen, however, that it is difficult to argue that we have a moral duty to create these institutions as long as we are operating with our traditional account of common sense morality and the related agency-centred account of responsibility. We need, in other words, to show that people have an obligation to create these institutions. There are a number of ways in which theorists do this in the literature on global justice. One prominent way – often deployed by theorists of a cosmopolitan bent – is to link responsibility directly to the production of justice and to view people as implicated, hence responsible, due to their participation in a common global basic structure.

In *Political Theory and International Relations*, Beitz argues that there is a duty of justice to the global poor, which may require the creation of institutions to dispense this obligation.[21] Beitz follows John Rawls in arguing that justice is "the first virtue" of social institutions, a view that confines questions of justice to the governing arrangement of particular societies. In contrast to Rawls, Beitz argues that the global order is constituted by a set of institutions and that membership in institutional systems is of moral relevance. Everyone across the globe is tied together under a shared institutional framework, and it is important that the background institutional framework in which we live is just. Using this Rawlsian line of reasoning, Beitz concludes that the principles of justice that applied (in Rawls's work) domestically should be extended to the global sphere. While this account does provide a good reason, rooted in a fundamental duty of justice, to create more just global institutions, this duty does not track individual responsibility or relate individual actions in the current unjust world to this obligation.

Another, quite distinct line of argument is deployed by Kok-Chor Tan and Simon Caney.[22] They have concentrated *not* on these empirical claims about the extent to which the globe now meets the conditions for a Rawlsian basic structure.[23] Instead, their arguments echo a luck egalitarian reading of Rawls's original argument for the difference principle in *A Theory of Justice*. Rawls's original position begins from the intuitive idea that a person's race, social class, natural endowments, and even religion are "arbitrary from a moral point of view" and that in a just order the effects of these should be nullified.[24] The original position, as a device of representation, asks people to imagine what principles they would agree to if they didn't know their actual status in society, their race or ethnic group, their natural endowments, or gender.[25] Since they are to agree to principles to govern the basic structure of their society as if they didn't know these features about themselves, the resulting principles are not biased by knowledge of "social contingencies." Similarly, luck egalitarianism, which is standardly applied to the domestic sphere, requires that people are compensated for undeserved bad luck – people who lack some fundamental natural endowments, suffer from accidents or illness, and/or are disadvantaged by social class. Distributive justice involves redistribution with an aim to mitigate the effects of these undeserved advantages, just as Rawls's difference principle is in part justified by the idea that talent itself is undeserved.

On this view, justice should *not* be understood as applying only when there is a "basic structure" or set of institutions in place. Rather, it is an institution-independent principle in the sense that the standards of justice give us an ideal by which to design and create institutions not yet in existence. As Kok-Chor Tan emphasizes, in this vein, the idea that justice depends on the existence of a set of institutions

> mistakenly inverts the relationship between justice and institutions. Justice aims to guide and regulate our existing institutions, and can call on us to create new ones if necessary. That is, justice constrains and informs our institutional arrangements, not the other way around. To tie justice to existing institutional schemes would be to misconstrue and pervert the purpose of justice.[26]

The luck egalitarian ideal has a natural global reach, for two reasons. First, it specifies a fundamental principle that not only governs the operation of principles but also is preinstitutional, requiring the setting up of institutions to meet the demands of equality. It requires us to establish equality of circumstances regardless of the empirical extent and role of institutions, regardless of whether they constitute a global basic structure, and regardless of the degree of interaction. This is a universalist and foundationalist argument for duties of justice, which, by definition, apply to all. Second, luck egalitarian theory seems particularly relevant to global justice because one of our core intuitions is that it is unfair that some people are simply born into poorer societies than others and, through no fault of their own, fare worse than others.

As Richard Arneson argues in defence of the luck egalitarian distributive ideal, the

> concern of distributive justice is to compensate individuals for misfortune.
> Some people are blessed with good luck, some are cursed with bad luck,
> and it is the responsibility of society – all of us regarded collectively – to
> alter the distribution of goods and evils that arise from the jumble of lot-
> teries that constitutes human life as we know it.[27]

Luck egalitarianism, unlike the Rawlsian basic structure argument,
relied on by Beitz, does have a very good account of responsibility,
whereby we are responsible for our choices, but not our circumstances;
responsible for the fruits of the exercise of autonomy, but not when our
fate is determined by a matter of good or bad luck. The problem with
this idea, when it is applied to the global level, is that on the larger
canvas of the global world, almost everything can be seen as a matter
of luck. This is because one could plausibly argue that the very society
that one is born into, which shapes one's opportunity sets, is a matter
of luck. As Thomas Nagel recognizes, the "accident of being born in a
poor rather than a rich country is as arbitrary a determinant of one's
fate as the accident of being born in to a poor rather than a rich family
in the same country."[28]

The problem with the first (Beitzian social structure) account is that
the duties of justice are specified in advance, from first principles, which
are said to be incumbent on everyone. It is ahistorical in that it does not
try to ascertain the webs of interaction and responsibility in which we
are situated. It is a-cultural in that it does not address the actual circumstances of our actions or beliefs. Although luck egalitarianism is different from this, in having an account of individual responsibility, the way
in which it has operated in the global justice literature has been to see
the very society that one lives in as a matter of (good or bad) luck. It is
good luck to be born in an affluent developed society; bad luck to be
born in a poor, developing country. Although the luck/circumstance
distinction is aimed at providing a sophisticated account of responsibility, this falls out of the global picture when the very country one is born
in or lives in is part of one's (good or bad) luck. These are not theoretical
problems,[29] but they do limit the theory's attractions for many social
movements. Indeed, social movements are concerned to argue not from
first principles of equality but from the idea that oppression is related to
the institutionally mediated actions of others and that many people are

involved in contributing to, perpetuating, and benefitting from oppression. For many people in the global South, and for many theorists of the global capitalist order, the luck egalitarian argument fails to address the historical fact of responsibility for current states of deprivation, injustice, and oppression.

Part Three: Young's Cosmopolitan Social Connection Model of Responsibility

Against this background Young's model can be seen as attempting both to show that there is an argument for the creation of more just institutions and practices and to base this argument on a backward-looking theory of responsibility for unjust outcomes. Young's social connection model provides just such a bridge. It bases our obligations to people in the global South on a theory that tracks our preinstitutional responsibility for this oppression. In her view, we have a duty to create new, more effective global institutions to solve the problem of global poverty. This is not simply an act of charity but a requirement of justice. It is a requirement of justice not because she thinks that Rawls's conditions for the "basic institutional structure" obtain at the global level, nor because it is conceived of as a requirement of a foundational principle of equality. Rather, the duty is based on a shared responsibility possessed by people embedded in chains of interaction with the global poor, which means that they can be held (partially) responsible for the current unjust state of affairs. Her focus is not on shared institutions nor on an argument that we have a global basic structure but on our *interaction* in oppressive processes.

In some ways, this model resembles Thomas Pogge's claim that one group is being harmed by the (institutionally mediated) actions of others. Pogge's argument, however, turns on the idea of "harm" compared to a baseline. It reinscribes the negative/positive duty distinction that is fundamental to Scheffler's and all traditional responsibility accounts. Pogge's argument, that is to say, attempts to demonstrate that the current global order is "harming" the poor, violating our negative duty not to harm others, rather than attempting to demonstrate a positive account of our duties to aid or rescue others. It begins from a standard libertarian starting point – namely, the no-harm principle.[30]

By contrast, Young focuses on the idea that people are embedded in many different systems of interaction, and through these interactions, we share responsibility in contributing to, perpetuating, and/or benefitting from oppression. To arrive at this general conclusion, she relies on two distinct, albeit related, arguments: one relating to the idea of structural injustice and the other to the idea of shared responsibility. She draws from Larry May's work on genocide to suggest ways in which our actions, and our interaction, make us responsible for alleviating the situation of the global order.

Structural injustice and structural inequality play a role in Young's theory of responsibility. The term "structure," which is central to the concept of "structural injustice," refers to the connections among varying positions in social space and their relationships. In her view, social positions are internally constituted through our relationships.[31] The fact that positions in social space are connected not only is important to her account of "structure" but also undergirds the claim that justice claims can be made at the global level, for the web of interaction encompasses everyone. According to Young,

> differing structural positions offer differing and unequal opportunities and potential benefits to their occupants, and their relations are such that constrained opportunities and minimal benefits for some often correlate with wider opportunities and minimal benefits for others.[32]

Social positions both influence and are influenced by the processes connecting them and this is important to conceptualizing the actors within the structure. However, Young is careful not to describe an overly deterministic approach, which would conceptualize the structure as operating in a way that completely determines the content, form, and structure of the positions in social space. She also claims to be sensitive to historicity. Accordingly, the conditions under which people act "are the products of previous actions, usually products of many coordinated and uncoordinated but mutually influencing actions."[33] In other words, the social structure is highly dynamic. It includes the relationships between the various positions in social space, the processes that connect and produce social positions, and the historical conditions that both enable and constrain these structural processes and positions.

Young combines this social structure account of the co-implicating nature of global justice with an account of responsibility, drawn from May's work on shared responsibility for genocide, which examines the conditions in which collective responsibility can be attributed. Young deploys the example of sweatshop labour in the global garment industry to illustrate both structural injustice and "shared responsibility." Anti-sweatshop activists have drawn attention to the poor conditions under which many garments of clothing are manufactured, and Young provides a theoretical account of how people are responsible because they are implicated through their interaction in the perpetuation of these unjust conditions. There is no doubt that the conditions are unjust. As she describes, the workers are subject to long, tedious, and oppressive work conditions. They are not permitted to leave their work station, even to take bathroom breaks. The buildings are often unsafe. The female garment workers are often subject to sexual harassment. Even liberal universalist accounts would argue that there are egregious injustices here, which need to be remedied, because basic human rights are violated. On a standard liberal human rights perspective, everyone has a moral duty to either not violate people's human rights or do what they can to protect human rights.

But Young's theory does not rely on a universalist account of the nature of the oppression. She focuses on the web of interaction and the way in which many people are implicated in the perpetuation of these conditions. Moreover, from the point of view of many of the people within the system, there is an important structural dimension to the perpetuation of oppressive conditions. As Young writes,

> each of the links in the chain [of manufacture and distribution] believes itself to be operating close to the margin in a highly competitive environment, and usually is under heavy pressure to meet orders at low costs by firms high up in the chain.[34]

In many cases, it is not only the consumer who is unaware of the conditions under which garments are produced. Others in the stratified and hierarchical system of production and distribution are unsure of the products that he/she purchases and/or distributes. In that sense, the people involved in these various positions are not morally responsible according to the traditional theory because, from the perspective of their own agency, they are not intending to commit these injustices or even knowledgeable about the garments that they buy.

Nevertheless, Young argues that their role in contributing to, benefiting from, and perpetuating the system makes them partially responsible. As Young, following May, argues, shared responsibility is an idea of personal responsibility, but "the person can be only personally responsible in a partial way, since he or she alone does not produce the outcomes."[35] Here, the emphasis is not on structures, but on the complex web of interactions that, together, produce the unjust outcome. Young makes it clear that this means that, since individuals share in creating the problem of exploitative working conditions, they also share a responsibility to find a way of correcting it. This may involve doing what they can, personally, to reduce their involvement in the global garment industry, and it may also involve activism to alter the structural conditions in which garment workers operate.

Part Four: Analysis and Critique

What can be said of Young's account, which emphasizes both one's own contribution (perpetuation and benefit) and the fact that this occurs within a structure of interaction? First, the problem with the structural model is that, to the extent that people can be seen or described as operating within structures which determine their choices and decisions, the scope of their responsibility is limited or restricted. Even Young admits this in her caveat that different people are differently positioned in social space, and one's own responsibility tries to track this social position. In practice, it seems to me that the powerful, who actually have control, autonomy, and possibly some opportunity for altering the social structure, are *more* responsible than the oppressed worker who had little alternatives and no possibility of changing the system. Indeed, as Scheffler first recognized, it would be unfair and wrong to attribute blame to someone for an injustice that he or she could not help if there were no genuine alternatives, no genuine scope for doing something else. We cannot be held morally responsible and/or remedially responsible for things that are beyond our control. To the extent that Young recognizes this, she departs from the structural model to suggest that within structures, some agents have more or less power, and therefore more scope for change or reform. To the extent that this argument recognizes that agency is an important element of responsibility, that people are responsible in so far as they are agents with choices, her account relies on the more traditional and plausible (because it is reflective of our sense of ourselves as agents) account articulated by Scheffler, among others.

Young does not only emphasize agency. She also argues that we are implicated in injustice if we benefit from that injustice. This idea – that benefitting from injustice creates responsibility – tends to cut against the foregoing analysis and to distinguish her account from a more traditional, agency perspective. However, it is not fully plausible to run together, as she does, creation, perpetuation, and benefit as grounding responsibility. Creation and perpetuation, especially when there is agency, are clear grounds for responsibility. But unsolicited benefit is less clear. Often, of course, the people who benefit from a system also have created or cocreated it, or at least work to perpetuate it, but in some cases, we can disentangle benefit from the foregoing and when we do, it is much less clear that there is any attached responsibility. Anwander has given the example of X-rays to illustrate exactly this point.[36] Anyone who has ever had an X-ray to check for a possible health problem benefits from a previous injustice, for the exact safe dose of radiation is known to us through scientific data gathered following the dropping of the atomic bomb on Hiroshima. Yet, although we benefit, it is doubtful whether there can be any responsibility on the part of people who have received X-rays. In other words, it is doubtful that mere unsolicited benefit creates responsibility; the real work in the account is on those actions that imply agency, just as Scheffler noted.

To see the attractions and limitations of Young's account, we should return to the three major global problems outlined in the first part of this chapter: exploitation, harms caused by multiple actors in complex webs of interactions, and collective harms. The global garment case runs together the first two. It is a case of exploitation as a result of complex interactions. As argued earlier, one of the major problems with the concept of exploitation is that it is difficult to arrive at a clear, conceptually independent account of exploitation. This is a problem not simply for Young but for all accounts of exploitation. Indeed, to the extent that Young makes use of the problem of severe injustice in the global garment case, the ethical issues can be captured by the severe and egregious violations of human rights.

Young, however, wants to say more than that people should endeavour to ensure that human rights everywhere are not violated. She seeks to tie responsibility to causal actions that implicate people in perpetuating or co-creating these unjust working conditions. This is an intuitively attractive and plausible move, but it is principally so to the extent that those people are co-implicated in these webs of interaction and have some alternatives and some choices. It is less plausible when we think of the impoverished single mother in the affluent West, who shops at Wal-Mart for cheap clothes to keep her children warm. When we imply that she is responsible as a consumer, it makes sense against a background of alternative choices. Here, we can see how the agency perspective seems to be tied, much closer than Young officially seems to suggest, to our conception of responsibility. Indeed, the concern with her account is that it gives less attention to agency than it should, and that that aspect of the traditional account of responsibility ought to be retained.

At the same time, the interactionist account that Young favours tends to suggest that people who are in a position to disengage from these webs of interaction, to live on a farm and weave their own wool, are "off the hook" so to speak with respect to the egregious violations of human rights that are ongoing all across the world. While this is not explicit in her account, it would seem to follow from the interactionist perspective that she adopts, and is problematic in so far as it suggests that we can disregard these injustices as long as we are not implicated in them. It is possible, however, that she avoids this through an empirical (but probably false) claim that we are all connected through webs of interaction. But this view, to the extent that it doesn't really try to track actual interactions, is not very compelling.

While Young's account does not seem to be much of a conceptual improvement over the traditional account of responsibility with respect to the first two kinds of global injustices, and indeed to rely implicitly on something like the traditional account of responsibility to track agency and positions in social space, her theory is much more compelling in the case of collective harms. I have argued in this chapter that the traditional theory of responsibility was unable to attribute responsibility in the case of collective harms – harms which were the result of a large (threshold) number of individuals, all acting in an uncoordinated way, producing harmful results, such as greenhouses gases, which contribute to global climate change. Yet there is clear evidence that greenhouse gases are an important causal element in global climate change, and people know that their actions contribute to greenhouse gases. The traditional theory does not ascribe responsibility for this because it is not a direct effect of an individual action. Young's theory takes the more plausible view that responsibility is shared because the harms are the result of many individual actions. Although this is less plausible in cases where the effects of individual actions are unpredictable and include not only effects of actions but also effects of failure to act, in the case of human-induced global climate change, the causal levers are well documented and scientifically established. The link to human action is clear and each individual can conceptualize his or her role in contributing to this harm. Young's theory, in contrast to the traditional theory, can ascribe responsibility to agents for the production of these gases, and so establish that we have an individual, personal responsibility to reduce them and a responsibility to work towards establishing institutions that are able to regulate and reduce them.

Conclusion

I have examined both Young's connection theory of responsibility and the traditional account of responsibility. I outlined three major problems for global justice and injustice – that is, exploitation, webs of interaction, and collective harms. I compared how they are addressed in both the traditional account of responsibility and Young's connection theory of responsibility. I argued that Young's theory implicitly relies on cognate concepts of agency to explain responsibility in cases of webs of interaction, and so does not offer a clear conceptual improvement over the traditional account, at least in dealing with the first two kinds of global injustices. However, the chapter also argued that it was more plausible as a theory of responsibility and more useful for dealing with collective harms, such as human-induced global climate change.

NOTES

1 The author is grateful to the Social Sciences Research Council of Canada for a research grant to fund this work, to Mira Bachvarova, Catherine Lu, and Katherine Mazurok for very incisive comments on the first draft of this chapter, and the audience at the Canadian Political Science association meeting, June 2009, where I presented an earlier version of this chapter. I am also grateful to Genevieve Fuji Johnson and Loralea Michaelis for helpful written comments, which have improved the text immensely.
2 Iris Marion Young, "Responsibility and Global Justice: A Social Connection Model," *Social Philosophy and Policy* 23, no. 1 (2006): 102–30. David Miller's *National Responsibility and Global Justice* (Oxford: Oxford University Press, 2007) also focuses on issues of responsibility in the global context, and I make use of some of his distinctions (between forward and backward-looking accounts of responsibility) here.
3 Interactionist approaches to justice include Charles Beitz, *Political Theory and International Relations* (Princeton, NJ: Princeton University Press, 1999), with a new afterword by the author.

4 I draw on Samuel Scheffler, *Boundaries and Allegiances: Problems of Justice and Responsibility in Liberal Thought* (Oxford: Oxford University Press, 2003). He has an excellent discussion of the phenomenological (agency) model.

5 Michael Green, "Institutional Responsibility for Global Problems," *Philosophical Topics* 30, no. 2 (Fall 2002): 84.

6 See Peter Singer, "Famine, Affluence and Morality," *Philosophy & Public Affairs* 1, no. 3 (Spring 1972): 229–43.

7 Ibid., 231.

8 Ibid.

9 Dale Jameson, "Duties to the Distant: Aid, Assistance, and Intervention in the Developing World," in *Current Debates in Global Justice*, ed. Gillian Brock and Darrel Moellendorf (Dordrecht, Netherlands: Springer, 2005), 151–70.

10 There are many cases where someone could act to aid X, so that they have the capacity to render a benefit, but this is not the end of the story, because there are important questions of (backward-looking) responsibility.

11 Such varied theorists as Thomas Pogge, *World Poverty and Human Rights* (Cambridge: Polity Press, 2002), 206, and Miller, *National Responsibility and Global Justice*, 266–7, appeal to some kind of nonexploitation principle. Interestingly, Miller is sensitive to the difficulties of calling the unfair process and unfair terms "exploitation."

12 There are a number of sophisticated recent Marxist accounts, which depart from that view – in particular, John Roemer, *A General Theory of Exploitation and Class* (Cambridge, MA: Harvard University Press, 1982), and Allen Wood, "Exploitation," *Social Philosophy and Policy* 12, no. 2 (1995): 136–58. Wood's theory denies that there is a link between exploitation and justice; and Roemer's theory identifies exploitation with what he calls the dominance condition, in which a group/class is exploited if there is a (hypothetically feasible) alternative, defined in terms of property relations (or control over the means of production) in which the group/class would have done better. This represents an alternative to the surplus labour theory of value conception, and Roemer attempts to show that exploitation so defined and class position are systematically related. See Chris Bertram, "A Critique of John Roemer's General Theory of Exploitation," *Political Studies* 36 (1988): 123–30.

13 For a very good analysis of the concept of exploitation on which this relies, see Alan Wertheimer, *Exploitation* (Princeton, NJ: Princeton University Press, 1996).

14 Christopher H. Wellman does have such a conception: he distinguishes exploitation from mere unfairness through the concept of rights. Christopher H. Wellman, *A Theory of Secession: The Case for Political Self-determination* (Cambridge: Cambridge University Press, 2005).

15 Note, however, that none of these accounts – even Scheffler's – can fully account for our views that some harmful but nonetheless predictable consequences are still legitimate – the market mechanism, for example, and the leaving of one's partner for personal reasons.

16 Thomas Pogge, "Severe Poverty as a Violation of Negative Duties," *Ethics & International Affairs* 19, no. 1 (2005): 17.

17 Scheffler, *Boundaries and Allegiances*, 43.

18 Green, "Institutional Responsibility," 87.

19 Young, "Responsibility and Global Justice," 103.

20 For an excellent discussion of institutional responsibility, and the superiority of institutions in dealing with global justice problems, including the collective harms discussed ahead, see Green, "Institutional Responsibility."

21 Beitz, *Political Theory and International Relations*.

22 Kok-Chor Tan, *Justice without Borders: Cosmopolitanism, Nationalism and Patriotism* (Cambridge: Cambridge University Press, 2004), and Simon Caney, *Justice beyond Borders: A Global Political Theory* (Oxford: Oxford University Press, 2005).

23 This does not preclude the possibility that theorists who are described here as developing an interactionist or institutional account might also make important use of luck egalitarian intuitions. In fact, both Beitz and Pogge do so, although I don't have space to show this here.

24 John Rawls, *A Theory of Justice* (Cambridge, MA: Harvard University Press, 1971), 15.

25 Gender was not one of the original arbitrary features, but Rawls added it to the list later on.

26 Tan, *Justice without Borders*, 34.

27 Richard Arneson, "Rawls, Responsibility and Distributive Justice," in *Justice, Political Liberalism, and Utilitarianisms: Themes from Harsanyi*, ed. Marc Fleurbaey, Maurice Salles, and John A. Weymark (Cambridge: Cambridge University Press, 2008), 32.

28 Thomas Nagel, "The Problem of Global Justice," *Philosophy & Public Affairs* 33, no. 2 (2005): 126.

29 I am also persuaded by some of the objections to luck egalitarianism put forward forcefully by Elisabeth Anderson, Jonathan Wolff, and Samuel Scheffler. In particular, I agree with Scheffler and Wolff that it is extremely difficult to distinguish between choices and circumstances and so luck

egalitarianism presupposes an impracticable theory of the person. They also argue that it can have negative indirect effects of being either too intrusive, thereby showing disrespect, or too harsh to those who have bad option luck. See Elisabeth S. Anderson, "What Is the Point of Equality?," *Ethics* 109, no. 2 (1999): 287–337; Jonathan Wolff, "Fairnesss, Respect and the Egalitarian Ethos," *Philosophy & Public Affairs* 27, no. 2 (1998): 97–122; and Samuel Scheffler, "What Is Egalitarianism?," *Philosophy & Public Affairs* 31, no. 1 (2003): 5–39.

30 The problem with this, and especially the moralized view of "harm" which Pogge relies on, is persuasively discussed in Alan Patten, "Should We Stop Thinking about Poverty in Terms of Helping the Poor?," *Ethics and International Affairs* 9, no. 1 (2005): 19–27.

31 Young, "Responsibility and Global Justice," 112.

32 Ibid.

33 Ibid., 113.

34 Ibid., 110.

35 Ibid., 122; Larry May, *Sharing Responsibility* (Chicago: University of Chicago Press, 1993), chapter 2. May's account differs from Young's in that he does not offer an unjust social structure account, but has a backward-looking conception of shared responsibility for harms or wrongs.

36 Norbert Anwander, "Contributing and Benefiting: Two Grounds for Duties to the Victims of Injustice," *Ethics & International Affairs* 19, no. 2 (2005): 39–45.

3 Power and Responsibility*

J.L. SCHIFF

Ours is a time of crisis. Much of the world confronts a serious economic and financial collapse, of which the recent implosion of the US housing market and huge job losses across that country are but two symptoms. This crisis has had far-reaching implications for ordinary Americans and for US domestic and foreign policy, and most recently has led to a downgrading of the US credit rating for the first time in almost a century. In addition, climate change – a problem famously neglected by the Bush administration – is once again being taken seriously as a threat to human and non-human forms of life. While there is considerable disagreement on the horizon of this threat, there is widespread consensus that a failure to act decisively could have profound implications. The commitment to adopt a framework for addressing climate change at the recent G-20 summit in Toronto reflects a growing awareness of this threat. Although they are matters of national and international policy, the problems of climate change and economic collapse share roots in the everyday activities of ordinary people all over the world: making and accepting loans that are beyond our means, producing and purchasing environmentally unfriendly products, failing to recycle,

* This chapter is a revised version of a paper presented at the Annual Meeting of the Canadian Political Science Association, Ottawa, 2009. It grows out of a larger project for which Young's work on political responsibility provides critical inspiration. The perspective on political responsibility that I develop herein is partly indebted to the work of Yusuf Has of the University of Chicago, though I develop it in a rather different direction. I thank Catherine Lu, Genevieve Fuji Johnson, Loralea Michaelis, and the rest of the participants in the Workshop on Political Responsibility for their comments on an earlier draft. Thanks of an entirely different order are due to Anna and Lia Schiff.

overconsuming energy, increasing carbon emissions, and so on. This situation demands a conception of shared political responsibility based upon the connections between our everyday activities and global political concerns. In one of her last published works, Iris Marion Young developed such a conception – the "social connection model of responsibility."[1] She developed this model to overcome the limitations of a "liability model of responsibility," which connects particular wrongful actions to specific harmful outcomes. Young claimed, rightly, that such a model is inadequate to the task of confronting problems to which individual contributions are less direct and traceable. In particular, the social connection model addresses problems of structural injustice. According to Young, we bear responsibility for such injustice when we contribute to processes that sustain it; and the appropriate response is to resist, protest, and subvert such processes. Her example is sweatshop labour, but I will show that her model is useful precisely because it encourages us to see climate change and financial crises *as* problems of injustice when we otherwise might not.

While I affirm the value of Young's model for conceptualizing responsibility for structural injustice,[2] I argue that the spirit of *shared* responsibility which she seeks to cultivate is undermined by something in both the social connection and liability models. Both implicitly rely too uncritically upon what I will call a "commodified" conception of power as a resource to be used instrumentally, towards particular ends. On this view, "having" power brings with it a corresponding responsibility to use it in a certain way. Those who lack power cannot be responsible. This position obscures the ways in which commodified power – that is, the resources at our disposal to effect change – can itself go misrecognized. One *reason* that the powerless cannot be responsible – a reason of which Young is clearly aware[3] – is that they are often deprived of the capacity to respond to their condition by seizing upon and using resources at their disposal. Their position of powerlessness can become misrecognized, a contingent condition that is experienced as a simple fact about the world. Moreover, positions of *privilege*, as much as positions of privation, may inhibit our capacity to respond because they too become naturalized and misrecognized. If the problems that we face demand urgent, collective responses, then we must ask a pressing question that notions of responsibility that share commodified conceptions of power tend to obscure: how can the capacities of human beings to respond to their condition be enhanced? Because Young's conception of structural injustice identifies different ways in which social and political arrangements can enhance some people's capacities at the expense of others, the conception of political responsibility she develops to address it provides a fruitful, but incomplete, starting point.

A full answer to my question is beyond the scope of this chapter, whose purpose is provisionally to stake out the terrain upon which we might answer it. Thinking about responsibility primarily in terms of commodified power obscures such questions, and bringing them to light requires us to rethink the relationship between power and responsibility. That is the task of this chapter. Specifically, I want to explore what it would mean to think about political responsibility in terms of constitutive, productive, and symbolic power. These forms of power are different from commodified power because they are not available for *use:* they are emergent, they circulate, they generate social positions and relations between them. Through a critical conversation with Hannah Arendt, Michel Foucault, and Pierre Bourdieu, I seek to develop a perspective on political responsibility from which the appropriate question is not just "Who is responsible and who is not?" but, rather, "How can we enhance our capacities to respond?" The well-known "capabilities" approach to social justice offers fertile ground for answers to that question. However, it seems inadequate to our globalized condition because it is insufficiently relational. It emphasizes various dimensions of individual and group flourishing and well-being, but neglects the kinds of relationships *between* individuals and groups that are at the root of structural injustice. Young's work on political responsibility provides that crucial relational dimension. By turning our attention to political responsibility as a capacity to respond we can bring a relational perspective to bear on the capabilities approach, while harnessing that approach for thinking about political responsibility.

The chapter proceeds as follows. In the first section, I argue that social connection and liability models share a commodified and instrumental conception of power that ultimately undermines the spirit of shared responsibility that admirably animates the former. This is so despite Young's earlier rejection of such a conception of power in favour of Hannah Arendt's constitutive conception of it as the ability to act in concert. Returning to that conception, I argue in the second section that while Arendt's understanding of power holds promise for a more widely shared political responsibility, she ultimately retains the problematic distinction between those who can be responsible and those who cannot, *and* she overlooks the problems of structural injustice that limit our sharing of responsibility. With a view to overcoming these problems, the next two sections turn towards disciplinary and symbolic power to ground political responsibility. In the third section, I show how Foucault's conception of disciplinary power illuminates the production of responsible subjects – that is, subjects with a capacity to respond. But this perspective crucially omits a means for those subjects to apprehend their condition of responsibility – that is, their implication in structural injustice. Accordingly in the fourth section, I argue that Pierre Bourdieu's conception of symbolic power helps both to explain Foucault's omission and to seek a way beyond it. Crises such as ours emerge as opportune moments at which to acknowledge our responsibility for structural injustice. In the final section, I suggest very briefly how we might draw critically upon the capabilities approach in order to theorize a capacity to respond in times of crisis and beyond.

Political Responsibility and the Limits of Commodified Power

Iris Marion Young's treatment of power as a commodity limits her thinking about political responsibility for structural injustice. Her treatment is implicit and unexpected. In an earlier essay Young had insisted, following Arendt, that (unlike violence) power is never a means to an end. *Rather* than being commodified and instrumental, power is emergent and *constitutive*. It is "the ability of persons jointly to constitute their manner of living together."[4] In her work on political responsibility, however, a commodified conception of power re-emerges surreptitiously. I am *not* seeking to banish questions of commodified power from discussions of political responsibility. Clearly our ability to assume our responsibility depends upon having the will and resources to do so. The problem is that Young is insufficiently attentive to some of the ways in which structural injustice obscures our abilities to make use of those resources. The perspective provided by a commodified account of power obscures this problem from the start.

When we ask questions about responsibility, we often have in mind some wrongful action (or omission) undertaken by an individual or group that harms another party and demands retrospective accounting. Both the wrong and the accounting can take different forms. If someone hits me without justification, I can take that person to court and try to prove that he or she hit me intentionally and wrongfully, and caused me some harm by doing so. If I am successful, I might secure some compensation, or else the responsible party might be deprived of his or her liberty. The same basic structure of holding another responsible appears in relations between groups as well. Germany was held responsible for causing World War I and was made to pay reparations, was forced to disarm, and so on. Both cases exemplify a standard account of causal responsibility,[5] which Young called a "liability model of responsibility."[6]

Such accounts of responsibility work when the connection between a wrongful action and a harmful outcome is relatively direct. But what happens when the link between actions and harms is much *less* direct, and when the harm in question is the result of actions that are not obviously wrongful but that constitute our most ordinary activities – like our purchasing decisions that sustain sweatshops or our use of fossil fuels and other technologies that can contribute to climate change? Young developed a model of responsibility that helps us think about those sorts of cases: the social connection model. She developed it in the context of what she calls "structural injustice." Young says that structural injustice "exists when social processes put large categories of persons under a systematic threat of domination or deprivation of the means to develop and exercise their capacities, at the same time as these processes enable others to dominate or have a wide range of opportunities for developing and exercising their capacities."[7] Her example is the sweatshop, where exploitation and domination are rampant.[8] Structural injustice is unlike a wrongful *individual* action. It "occurs as a consequence of many individuals and institutions" pursuing their interests "within given institutional rules and accepted norms." In her terms, "all the persons who participate … in the ongoing schemes of cooperation that constitute these structures are responsible for them" because "they are part of the process that causes them."[9]

Standard models of responsibility are inadequate for conceptualizing responsibility for structural injustice because they "require that we trace a direct relationship between the action of an identifiable person or group and a harm."[10] For that task, the "liability model of responsibility" is appropriate. We assign responsibility to an agent or agents whose faulty actions are causally connected to a harm, as long as those actions were undertaken voluntarily "and performed with adequate knowledge of the situation."[11] When structural processes produce injustice, however, "in most cases [this] is not possible," and the social connection model becomes useful. In this model, "individuals bear responsibility for structural injustice because they contribute by their actions to the processes that produce unjust outcomes."[12] Responsibility comes not from the nature and effects of our particular actions, but "from belonging together with others in a system of interdependent processes of cooperation and competition through which we seek benefits and aim to realize projects."[13] Unlike responsibility under the liability model, responsibility based on social connection can be discharged only collectively. Thus, responsibility for structural injustice is ultimately *political*.[14]

While Young develops her model around the example of sweatshop labour – which, because it is exploitative and oppressive, is readily recognizable as a problem of injustice – her model encourages us to view *other* global problems as problems of injustice as well. Climate change is a problem that, in principle, affects everyone. But it affects different groups of people differently, because wealthier countries can more easily respond by "going green" than can poorer countries, for which changes in economic production and consumption come at a higher cost. So while environmentally unfriendly practices may ultimately affect everyone, they do seem to

> put large categories of persons under a systematic threat of … deprivation of the means to develop and exercise their capacities, at the same time as these processes enable others to … have a [wider] range of opportunities for developing and exercising their capacities.[15]

As for global financial crises, it needs hardly to be said that not only are some people currently suffering *much* more than others, but also some, like "predator lenders," have even *benefitted* from the crisis. Thus, Young's social connection model enables us to see a wider range of global problems as problems of structural injustice.

While Young's model enlarges our view of what counts as structural injustice, one feature of that model undermines its spirit. A purpose of the social connection model is to emphasize the *shared* nature of political responsibility for structural injustice. But the extent of that sharing is carefully, if quietly, circumscribed. Those who contribute to the processes that produce injustices "have responsibilities to work to remedy" them.[16] By implication, those who suffer injustice are not responsible for the conditions that bring it about. This position has intuitive appeal in a case like sweatshop labour, where the oppression and domination are quite evident, and where we would certainly not want to say that the exploited are responsible for their own exploitation. It is perhaps less clear but no less appealing in cases like climate change and financial crises. While those who unduly bear the burdens of climate change and financial crises might also have contributed to the processes that sustain each of those phenomena, it is unreasonable, perhaps even cruel, to insist that they bear the same responsibilities for their condition as those for whom the burdens of sharing the world in common are lighter. And yet, to the extent that we *do* share the world in common, there is something troubling in a conception of political responsibility that presumptively limits that sharing *only* to those who benefit from it. The presence of suffering does not automatically entail the absence of responsibility.

Arendt identifies this troubling aspect of collective responsibility in the context of statelessness. While arguing that we are politically responsible for acts undertaken by our state – and therefore in our name – Arendt allows that there is "a category of men who [are] truly outcasts, belonging to no internationally recognizable community whatever, the refugees and stateless people, who indeed cannot be held politically responsible for anything." "It is precisely this absolute innocence," Arendt observes, "that condemns them to a position outside, as it were, of mankind as a whole."[17] Now neither sweatshop workers nor perhaps most of victims of structural injustice are stateless per se, although their plight is sometimes overlooked in ways that suggest otherwise. Yet Young's thinking about political responsibility threatens to put them in a structurally similar position. They are not politically responsible and, to that extent, are condemned to be outside of any national or (nascent) global community.

How does this result come about? How does a conception of political responsibility that emphasizes sharing and connection end up limiting that sharing and reinforcing the disconnection of many human beings from the conditions of their existence? This troubling implication of Young's model grows out of something that it *shares* with the liability model she so perceptively criticizes. Both depend for their practical weight upon a commodified conception of power – that is, of power as a resource to be possessed and used in relation to other people. We are held liable (or are responsible under the terms of Young's social connection model) because we have the power to make a difference, for good or for ill. In both conceptions, with great power comes great responsibility. Those who "have" more power have the responsibility to mitigate society's ills. Those who lack power do not. The current preponderance of American power has reinforced for many the notion that such power must be exercised responsibly – though interpretations of what that means vary wildly – while irresponsible exercises of that power deserve some sort of censure. Such claims track a liability model of responsibility. In the context of structural injustice, the role of commodified power is less to wield it for or against others than to accumulate it in order to insulate *oneself* from the vicissitudes of global social, political, and economic processes. It can also, of course, be used to exploit the vulnerabilities of others in the face of such processes, as we have seen to such great and calamitous effect in the US mortgage crisis. Here too, with great power comes great responsibility. Those who contribute to the processes that produce injustice (and are often themselves insulated from it) have a responsibility to remedy the injustice done to those who lack the power to insulate themselves from or resist it. The implication, in both models, is this: those who "have" power can be responsible, and those who "lack" it cannot be. Such a distinction undermines the project of expanding the scope of our shared responsibility for global problems by presumptively identifying who can be responsible and who cannot.

A familiar way of characterizing the problem here is to say that commodified power in its various forms is too unevenly distributed. If we want responsibility to be distributed more evenly, then we need a correspondingly more egalitarian distribution of power – a dramatic restructuring of global resources that would put more power, and thus more responsibility, into more hands. But such a calculus ignores an important feature of structural injustice. As I have argued in more detail elsewhere, structural injustice is hard to respond to because it is a product of such ordinary activities – like buying clothes, disposing of waste, borrowing and lending, and so on – that their connection to global problems is difficult to notice.[18] It is easy not to think about those connections (the problem of thoughtlessness), or to deceive ourselves about them (the problem of bad faith), *or* to not even see them at all. As our world takes on the trappings of a natural and taken-for-granted, rather than social and therefore contingent, condition, we may no longer recognize the connections between our ordinary activities and the persistence of structural injustice (the problem of misrecognition).[19] These dispositions, which tend to conceal from us our connections to problems of structural injustice, likewise tend to conceal the discrepancies in commodified power that make some vulnerable to such injustice while insulating others. Thus such discrepancies get reconceived and reconstituted, not as problems of power, but as matters of good versus ill fortune, of industry versus idleness or, at the limit, simply as the way things are. Such reconfigurations militate against a global redistribution of resources because they militate against seeing the problem of structural injustice *as* a problem of power to begin with. Thus they make it difficult to respond to global injustice in its various forms. The commodified conception of power that underlies Young's account of political responsibility obscures these conceptual and practical limitations. Addressing them requires a broader perspective on the relationships between power and responsibility. We need a conception of power not as a resource to be used, but as the productive source of capacities to be cultivated – like the capacity to respond to one's condition. That would enable us to ask not just, "Who is responsible for injustice and who is not?" but also, "How can we enhance our capacities to respond to such injustice?"

Constitutive Power and Political Responsibility

We can begin to trace the emergence of such a conception of power in the work of Hannah Arendt, whose thinking about power animated Young's earlier work. In the aftermath of totalitarian domination, whose chief features were terror and isolation,[20] Arendt argued that power is always potential and is actualized in the public realm. "Power is always, as we would say, a power potential, and not an unchangeable, measureable, and reliable entity … [it] springs up between men when they act together and vanishes the moment they disperse."[21] Power is never a resource to be used towards some end. Such commodified instrumentality is reserved for faculties like "strength" and "force," for which Arendt reserves the terms "possession" and "application."[22] In an incisive critique of Hobbes, Arendt even suggests that totalitarian domination is the logical conclusion of his commodified and instrumental view of power. She notes that "for some three hundred years there was neither a sovereign who would 'convert this speculation [about the limitless acquisition of power] into the Utility of Practice,' nor a bourgeoisie politically conscious and economically mature enough openly to adopt Hobbes' philosophy of power."[23] That philosophy, for Arendt, was a condition of totalitarianism. In order to reclaim power philosophically and politically *against* totalitarianism, then, power had to be something other than a resource to be accumulated and used. It is a capacity that emerges when human beings act together. And, unlike instrumental power, this "constitutive power" can never be a source of omnipotence that insulates its possessor from the vicissitudes of life among others. Its status as potentiality only occasionally actualized, its dependence upon the presence of others, makes it too fragile for that. Power, for Arendt, is nothing more or less than that fragile potentiality to act in concert.

There is something in Arendt's conception of power that resonates with my concern about a more expansive sharing in political responsibility. In her writing on totalitarianism, Arendt became preoccupied with the problem of isolation, and its attendant loneliness. Power can overcome isolation because it can *only* emerge when human beings are together and act in concert. The actualization of its potentiality *is* such being-together. This gives us one resource to overcome that distinction between those who are responsible and those who are not that is so detrimental to sharing responsibility. In Arendtian terms, power appears in those moments when we come together to acknowledge and confront global structural injustice. That appearance of power brings with it a capacity to respond in concert to our condition.

If Arendt's approach to power is initially encouraging, two dimensions of her approach to political responsibility that follow from it seem to undermine the effort to conceptualize a more expansive notion of the latter. The first is that as we have already seen, Arendt's conception of responsibility is explicitly territorial in character. That is why stateless peoples are so problematic for her, and why they cannot be responsible for anything. Such a territorialized view of responsibility militates against a more globally shared responsibility for injustice. Elsewhere Arendt underscores this territorialization of responsibility. In "Collective Responsibility," her paradigmatic example of political responsibility is that which citizens bear for the actions undertaken in their name, by their state. She asserts that we

> can escape this political and strictly collective responsibility only by leaving the community, and since no man can live without belonging to some community, this would simply mean to exchange one community for another and hence one kind of responsibility for another.[24]

The second problem is closely related: when she insists that people are responsible for actions undertaken in their name, she is oddly indifferent to the structures of both privilege and exclusion that characterize political life[25] and that are the basis of claims about structural injustice. Such structures of privilege and exclusion make it difficult to claim that a community's activity speaks for all of its members. The only options available then are either to ignore those structures, as Arendt mostly seems to, or to contest and resist them. Taking the latter course, working against structures of privilege and exclusion, helps to change the question of political responsibility to: how can we enhance our capacities to respond to our condition? In the remainder of this chapter, I frame this problem in terms of two related questions about power. First, how are individuals produced as responsible subjects? And second, given the ordinariness of our contributions to global structural injustice, how can it become an object of response at all?

Power and the Production of Responsible Subjects

In exploring the role of power in the production of subjects, we can take our lead from Michel Foucault. Against the model of sovereign power associated with Thomas Hobbes's *Leviathan* – exemplified, for instance, in the emblazoning of itself publicly upon the bodies of criminals through torture in the eighteenth century[26] – Foucault posits "another way to go further toward a new economy of power relations."[27] Against sovereign power held by individuals (or groups) and applied through force, Foucault argues that the "exercise of power" is "a way in which certain actions modify others."[28] Foucault seeks not to replace juridical power but to supplement it with a conception of disciplinary power that clarifies the micropractices of the former. Disciplinary power, for Foucault, refers to the action *of* actions *upon* actions. Circulating in social and political space, yet wielded by no one, disciplinary power "does not act directly and immediately upon others. Instead, it acts upon their actions,"[29] making some thinkable and possible, and others unthinkable and impossible. By disengaging a conception of power from questions of who *holds* it (which is precisely what I want to do with respect to questions of political responsibility), Foucault shifts the discussion towards *how* power works. Through this shift he arrives at his famous conception of power as ubiquitous, hidden, capillary, and so on. Rather than being wielded, power *circulates* or *operates* (but, importantly, is *not* circulated or operated). And the upshot of such a conception is that, unlike the sovereign, repressive model of power, for Foucault, power is *productive* in several respects:

> This form of power applies itself to immediate everyday life, which categorizes the individual, marks him by his own individuality, attaches him

to his own identity, imposes a law of truth on him ... It is a form of power that makes individuals subjects.[30]

Subjects, in short, are *effects* of power. More precisely, subjects are produced by disciplinary power. Foucault connects the disciplines closely to the regulation of the body. This regulation of the body in prisons gradually replaced the spectacle of public torture that prevailed in eighteenth-century France and elsewhere.[31] With the development of prisons the body as such was no longer the locus of punishment – rather, that locus became the soul. And the technique visited upon the soul was that of regulation, correction, and teaching, and no longer a technique of physical brutality. In its new mode, punishment becomes "a political technology of the body."[32] Its regulation is achieved through discipline, a set of practices enabled by the heightened visibility exemplified by Bentham's panopticon. The panopticon, the all-seeing eye, enables the regulation of bodies through "hierarchical observation," "normalizing judgment," and "examination."[33] The effect of discipline is the production of "docile bodies," bodies that are moulded according to rules and then internalize these rules and effectively become their own overseer.[34] In the carceral society, discipline becomes internalized. The panopticon, that only-conceived, and thus largely invisible, observatory, becomes a ubiquitous regulatory principle in society.[35]

All of this sounds very ominous. Disciplinary power operates through specific institutionalized and internalized practices to produce docile, governable subjects. And indeed one can tell a story about structural injustice that takes this shape: trained in the disciplines of capitalism and "freedom," trained to view the less fortunate as lazy or unlucky, individuals come to participate in regular, even regulated ways in the maintenance of systems that promote structural injustice, whether in the area of global capitalism – such as the purchase of cheap sweatshop goods – or in the area of global environmental problems, such as environmentally unfriendly building practices, failure to recycle, and so on. What's more, insofar as giving short shrift to environmental concerns often serves the interests of global capitalism, these two disciplines are mutually reinforcing. The practices that constitute global capitalism thus discipline us to reproduce structural injustice on a global scale.

Such a view of disciplinary power is totalizing indeed, and Foucault has frequently been taken to task for leaving little room for creative

54   J.L. Schiff

resistance to the normalizing effects of discipline (even as he insists that
they are both possible and ever-present).[36] But why must discipline produce docility in the face of injustice? Might not a different discipline, a
different constellation of regulated practices, give rise to a militant resistance to those practices that sustain global injustice? Such practices
would, in Foucault's terms, produce responsible subjects. Both the anti-
sweatshop and environmental movements offer preliminary examples
of sites of power that produce not docile but militant and responsible
subjects. These movements are institutions in the loose sense of being
collectivities united by a particular constellation of aims – not to punish but to contest structures of domination and consumption, and to
mobilize others to join the struggle through educating the public about
those structures and their effects. By drawing upon and reproducing a
discourse of structural injustice, such entities participate in the production, in the disciplining, of subjects ready to respond to conditions of
structural injustice. The makings of response-able subjects are already
immanent in contemporary life.

Symbolic Power and the Capacity to Respond

But disciplinary power, in its production of responsible subjects, leaves
an important question unanswered: how does structural injustice become a problem *for me*? It is one thing for the exploitation and domination of human beings to present themselves as problems that demand
a response, and for me to be a subject capable of responding to it. But
what is it that makes *my* everyday activities a meaningful part of any
response? Disciplinary power only prepares a subject capable of responding to global structural injustice. It does not yet make responding
a practically meaningful part of her everyday experience. In order for
that to happen, something needs to expose the connection between our
everyday activities and the persistence of structural injustice, which
otherwise tends to go misrecognized. What gets misrecognized in this
case is the operation of what Pierre Bourdieu calls "symbolic power."
Such power is disrupted in moments of crisis, which reveal the domi-
native and exploitative foundations of political orders that tend to be
taken for granted.

   In the course of everyday life, according to Bourdieu, we make our
way in the world mostly according to unreflective habit, or what Bourdieu calls *habitus*, which connects objective structures of social and
political life to the dispositions that actualize and "tend to reproduce

them."[37] A *habitus* is a "durably installed generative principle of regulated improvisation," an "immanent law ... laid down in each agent
by his earliest upbringing."[38] It is productive and reproductive because
the practices it produces tend to reproduce the objective conditions of
existence.[39] It is essential for social life because it produces "a common-
sense world endowed with the *objectivity* secured by consensus on the
meaning ... of practices and the world." Furthermore, the "homogene-
ity of habitus is what ... causes practices and works to be immediately
intelligible and foreseeable, and hence taken for granted."[40] Habitus
makes the world make sense to us. It does so without explicit rules or
coordination, "without presupposing a conscious aiming at ends or an
express mastery of the operations necessary to attain them."[41] Habitus
operates unconsciously. And the unconscious, according to Bourdieu,
is "never anything other than the forgetting of history which history
itself produces by incorporating the objective structures it produces in
the second nature of habitus."[42] Thus a habitus is "history turned into
nature, i.e. denied as such."[43] To put this in more concrete terms, there
is a habitus involved in being a political subject under the conditions of
global capitalism, and that habitus makes us look much like Foucault's
disciplined subjects. Just as Foucault recognizes the historicity of any
particular discipline, Bourdieu is acutely aware of the historicity, the
contingency of any particular habitus. And while Foucault identifies
discipline as the mechanism that produces and normalizes the activities of political subjects, Bourdieu assigns that role to misrecognition.
It is ultimately misrecognition that guarantees the taken-for-granted
character of everyday life, the seeming naturalness of a global order in
which some are systematically advantaged while others are disadvantaged. As the global order takes on the appearance of nature, it becomes
increasingly difficult to see how we might respond to it and, indeed, to
see that there *is* something to which we might respond.

Misrecognition is central to the maintenance of systems of domination and exploitation. "Every established order," Bourdieu insists,
"tends to produce (to very different degrees and with very different
means) the naturalization of its own arbitrariness."[44] It does so through
the reproduction of systems of classification, such as sex, age or class,
which "[reproduce] ... the power relations of which they are the product, by securing the misrecognition, and hence the recognition, of the
arbitrariness upon which they are based."[45] Thus misrecognized, "the
natural and social world appears as self-evident," an experience that
Bourdieu calls *doxa*. Misrecognition naturalizes existing social and

political orders so that we tend to take them for granted rather than to question them. Thus, rather than appearing to us as a problem to which we can respond, misrecognition makes structural injustice look like a more or less immutable, even natural, fact about the world, unconnected to any of our ordinary activities. It simply "is."

This persistence of misrecognition, which underwrites the experience of ordinary life and renders unproblematic conditions of structural injustice, is itself an effect of power. But rather than disciplinary power which produces and reproduces subjects, misrecognition is sustained by *symbolic power*, whose operation produces and reproduces naturalized social and political structures. Symbolic power is similar to disciplinary power, in that it is not commodified but productive. Further, like disciplinary power, symbolic power is more elusive and amorphous than commodified power, which is always held *by* someone and used *for* some purpose. But there is a crucial difference between them. Whereas for Foucault disciplinary power circulates anywhere and everywhere, yet is apparently wielded by no one, Bourdieu is explicitly critical of such a view. He might as well be writing about Foucault when he says that

> in a state of the field in which power is visible everywhere, while in previous ages people refused to recognize it even when it was staring them in the face [an effect of misrecognition, perhaps?], it is perhaps useful to remember that, *without turning power into a "circle whose centre is everywhere and nowhere"* … we have to be able to discover it in places where it is *least visible*, where it is *most completely misrecognized*.[46]

One can hear in this call a criticism of disciplinary power, which tends to be everywhere and nowhere and thus *appear* completely agentless. Indeed, Bourdieu suggests that to imagine power without an agent is to misrecognize the very idea and operation of power. Thus he claims that what sustains social and political structures is symbolic power. Taking the form primarily of ideological systems, such power "can be exercised only with the complicity of those who do not want to know that they are subject to it or even that they themselves exercise it."[47] Symbolic power operates effectively when and because it is misrecognized as the absence of power. Through the working of symbolic power – in which we are complicit, not because we "possess" it, but because we maintain the structures that support it – the social and political world appears unproblematic and self-evident. Symbolic power makes structural injustice into just a fact of life.

What, then, is to be done? What might disrupt both the subjectifying processes of disciplinary power and the ideological misrecognition underwritten by symbolic power so that subjects are capable of responding in practically meaningful ways to the problem of global structural injustice? Bourdieu, for one, assigns such a role to what he calls crises, moments of radical disruption in which our ordinary ways of being and doing cease to function. If the role of the *habitus* is to bring objective and subjective structures into accord, what Bourdieu calls an "objective crisis ... [breaks] the immediate fit between the subjective structures and the objective structures"[48] – that is, it renders an existing habitus unworkable by disrupting the practical context it helped to navigate. In moments of crisis, our ordinary ways of getting along in the world suddenly seem not to work. In breaking the fit between subjective and objective structures, crises "destroy self-evidence practically. It is when the social world loses its character as a natural phenomenon that the question of the natural or conventional character ... of social facts can be raised."[49] Crises can bring the undiscussed, that which is typically taken for granted, into discussion. Indeed, "there is perhaps no better way of *making felt* the real function of classificatory systems" – like class systems, for instance, or more broadly the social, political, economic, and spatial organization of our world – "than to evoke as concretely as possible the abrupt and total transformation of daily life."[50]

Because they compel us to acknowledge what we ordinarily take for granted, crises provide occasions for overcoming misrecognition and the symbolic power that underwrites it. For Bourdieu, this happens most powerfully when the dominated "[reject] the definition of the real that is imposed upon them through logical structures reproducing the social structures" and "[lift] the (institutionalized or internalized) censorships which it implies." At this point, classificatory schemes hitherto taken for granted "become the object and instrument of class struggle." Once what has been tacit becomes speakable, "it becomes necessary to undertake the work of conscious systematization and express rationalization which marks the passage from doxa to orthodoxy."[51] Once the taken-for-granted, implicit rules that structure our relations to others are questioned, they must be defended. And the necessity of defence implies the existence of other possibilities, what Bourdieu calls the heterodox "existence of *competing possibles*." Crises allow us to reimagine our relations to other people, to respond to them in the way that our condition demands and that misrecognition tends to obstruct. What this means, from our point of view, is that our contemporary moment, with its confluence of patent and latent crises, is also a moment of significant opportunity – to reconfigure our economic and environmental activities in ways that could mitigate structural injustice. While a misrecognized world often presents itself as a *fait accompli*, a world in crisis may open up possibilities not only *for* response but also for debate about and development of measures that might improve human beings' capacities to respond in the face of global structural injustice, and thus to share responsibility for the unjust suffering of others.

The Capacity to Respond and the Capabilities Approach

Before concluding, I want to point out that framing the question of political responsibility in terms of the capacity to respond recalls an important way of thinking about problems of justice: the "capabilities approach." Young's own formulation of the problem of structural injustice, with its reference to people's "means to develop and exercise their capacities," carries echoes of this way of thinking. Developed by Amartya Sen and extended by Martha Nussbaum and others, the capabilities approach rejects both utilitarian and Rawlsian ideals of human welfare in favour of an emphasis on human flourishing or well-being.[52] In one formulation, Sen puts it this way: "The capability approach to a person's advantage is concerned with evaluating it in terms of his or her actual ability to achieve various valuable functions as a part of living." Those individual level evaluations then become the basis for an "aggregative appraisal as well as for the choice of institutions and policy." This approach concerns, first, an individual's "functionings ... the various things that he or she manages to do or be in leading a life. The *capability* of a person reflects the alternative combinations of functionings the person can achieve, and from which he or she can choose one collection."[53] The functionings from which a person can choose – assuming she is an environment in which she *can* choose – vary from "elementary" ones such as nourishment, to more "complex" ones, like "achieving self-respect or being socially integrated."[54] From this point of view, justice is a matter of ensuring that individuals are capable of being and doing as they will, of leading the life they choose. A capabilities approach is thus intimately connected with the achievement of some sort of positive freedom.

This valuable picture of human capabilities overlooks the relationships *between* capabilities that are manifest in problems of structural injustice. Some individual or group's capacity to "achieve various valuable functions" is often bought at the expense of others. That is the very *definition* of structural injustice. But while the capabilities approach emphasizes the capabilities of individuals or groups (and rightly seeks to enhance them) it neglects the *relationships* between individuals and groups as important sites for the development of a particular capacity – namely, the capacity to respond to our condition. The point here is not just to suggest, as many have before, that the range of relevant capabilities needs to be expanded to include the capacity to respond. Rather, the point is that the capacity to respond is central to the project of freedom that animates the capabilities approach. Without it, the capabilities approach is blind to the problem of structural injustice, which is a significant impediment to human freedom. Or, to put it differently, what the capabilities approach does not recognize is the interconnection of human freedom and the development of political responsibility.

Conclusion

Ours is a time of crisis that reveals unexpected sites of structural injustice. In order to properly confront crises such as economic collapse and climate change, we need to recognize two things: first, that these crises must be confronted collectively; and second, that burdens of these crises are distributed unevenly. These features of our contemporary moment call for shared responsibility. Indeed, Young made it clear that political responsibility for such injustice *must* be shared. In this chapter I have argued that her unique account of political responsibility, the social connection model, undermines that spirit of sharing by relying too uncritically upon a commodified conception of power. I have suggested that sharing responsibility more adequately requires that we rethink the relationship between responsibility and power. Without letting go of commodified power, which is crucial for combating injustice, I have surveyed several other conceptions of power – constitutive, disciplinary, and symbolic – that may point in a fruitful direction. Instead of forcing us to pose the question of political responsibility in terms of who is responsible and who is not, these forms of power suggest new questions: How can we enhance our capacities to respond? How can we make it possible for more people – especially those whom

Arendt and Young implicitly exclude from occupying the position of responsible subjects – to find and use resources necessary to confront the burdens of economic collapse, climate change, and other crises that may yet come? Sharing political responsibility demands that we answer these questions together.

NOTES

1 Iris Marion Young, "Responsibility and Global Justice: A Social Connection Model," *Social Philosophy & Policy* 23, no. 1 (2006): 102–30, http://dx.doi.org/10.1017/S0265052506060043.
2 But see my sympathetic critique in Jacob Schiff, "Confronting Political Responsibility: The Problem of Acknowledgment," *Hypatia* 23, no. 3 (2008): 99–117.
3 See Iris Marion Young, *Justice and the Politics of Difference* (Princeton, NJ: Princeton University Press, 1990); Iris Marion Young, *Inclusion and Democracy* (Oxford, UK: Oxford University Press, 2001).
4 Iris Young, *Global Challenges: War, Self-determination and Responsibility for Justice* (New York: Polity, 2007), 84–5. Cf. Hannah Arendt, *On Violence* (New York: Harcourt, Brace, and World, 1969).
5 See, e.g., Joel Feinberg, *Doing and Deserving: Essays in the Theory of Responsibility* (Princeton, NJ: Princeton University Press, 1975).
6 Young, "Responsibility and Global Justice," 116.
7 Ibid.
8 This definition of structural injustice reflects its ancestry in Young's early critique of distributive theories of justice. In *Justice and the Politics of Difference*, Young argues that injustice ought to be understood not just in terms of uneven material distributions, but also in terms of "oppression" and "domination," both of which exceed material conditions in their scope and include "institutional processes" and "conditions" that prevent people from engaging in various forms of self-determination and self-development (*Justice and the Politics of Difference*, 38).
9 Young, "Responsibility and Global Justice," 114.
10 Ibid.
11 Ibid., 116; see also Feinberg, *Doing and Deserving*.
12 Young, "Responsibility and Global Justice," 119.
13 Ibid.
14 Ibid., 116.
15 Ibid.

16 Ibid., 103.
17 Hannah Arendt, "Collective Responsibility," in *Responsibility and Judgment,* ed. Jerome Kohn (1968; New York: Schocken Books, 2005), 150.
18 Schiff, "Confronting Political Responsibility."
19 Ibid.
20 Hannah Arendt, *The Origins of Totalitarianism* (San Diego: Harcourt, 1948), esp. part 3, "Totalitarianism."
21 Hannah Arendt, *The Human Condition* (Chicago: University of Chicago Press, 1998), 200.
22 For a more detailed account of Arendt's distinction between strength, force, and power, see Arendt, *On Violence.*
23 Arendt, *Origins of Totalitarianism,* 143.
24 Arendt, "Collective Responsibility," 150.
25 See, e.g., Iris Marion Young, *Inclusion and Democracy* (Oxford: Oxford University Press, 2000).
26 Michel Foucault, *Discipline and Punish: The Birth of the Prison* (New York: Vintage Books, 1995), 3–6.
27 Michel Foucault, "The Subject and Power," in *Michel Foucault: Beyond Structuralism and Hermeneutics,* 2nd ed., ed. Hubert L. Dreyfus and Paul Rabinow (Chicago: University of Chicago Press, 1982), 210.
28 Foucault, "The Subject and Power," 219.
29 Ibid., 220.
30 Ibid., 212.
31 Foucault, *Discipline and Punish.*
32 Ibid., 30.
33 Ibid., 170–92.
34 Ibid., 135–69.
35 Ibid., 293–308.
36 See, e.g., Duccio Trombadori, introduction to *Remarks on Marx* by Michel Foucault (New York: Semiotexte, 1991), 15–25; Nancy Fraser, "Foucault on Modern Power: Empirical Insights and Normative Confusions," *Praxis International* 3(1981): 272–87; and Jürgen Habermas, *The Philosophical Discourse of Modernity* (Cambridge, MA: MIT, 1987). For a critique of this position, see Brent L. Pickett, "Foucault and the Politics of Resistance," *Polity* 28 (1996): 445–66.
37 Pierre Bourdieu, *Outline of a Theory of Practice* (Cambridge: Cambridge University Press, 1977), 3.
38 Ibid., 78, 81.
39 Ibid., 78.
40 Ibid., 80.

41 Ibid., 72.
42 Ibid., 78–9.
43 Ibid., 78.
44 Ibid., 164.
45 Ibid.
46 Pierre Bourdieu, *Language and Symbolic Power* (Cambridge, MA: Harvard University Press, 1991), 163.
47 Ibid., 164.
48 Bourdieu, *Outline of a Theory of Practice*, 168–9.
49 Ibid., 169.
50 Ibid., 159.
51 Ibid., 169.
52 See, e.g., John M. Alexander, *Capabilities and Social Justice: The Political Philosophy of Amartya Sen and Martha Nussbaum* (London: Ashgate, 2007).
53 Amartya Sen, "Capability and Well-being," in *The Quality of Life*, ed. Martha Nussbaum and Amartya Sen (Oxford: Clarendon, 1993), 30–1.
54 Ibid., 31.

4 Autonomous Development and Global Empowerment

NANCY BERTOLDI

Inspired by the emergence and transformative potential of a transnational public sphere, Iris Marion Young tackled problems of global justice in her later essays, with interesting implications for conceptualizing political responsibility beyond borders.[1] In these works, Young engaged with issues as wide-ranging as the Israeli-Palestinian peace process, the wars in Afghanistan and Iraq, trends in American foreign policy, the NATO intervention in Kosovo, the global anti-sweatshop movement, and aboriginal self-governance.

In this chapter, I bring together diverse aspects of Young's work to construct a new paradigm of "autonomous development" that can support a feminist agenda of global empowerment. This agenda calls for the elimination of oppressive forces frequently impeding the autonomy of women and men worldwide. It seeks to enable persons to realize their autonomy as relationally interconnected agents.

The paradigm of autonomous development has four conceptual dimensions: it is grounded in a relational conception of agency; it requires the elimination of oppression and domination in social relations; it emphasizes the need to evaluate social institutions in structural terms; and it posits a model of political responsibility that points beyond mere liability. All four dimensions of autonomous development highlight the social constitution of agency and the significance of the broader social context within which this occurs.

After outlining the main tenets of the paradigm of autonomous development that Young's thought makes available, I flesh out how it influences her treatments of democratic citizenship and global justice. At the domestic level, scrutinizing the specific case of the United States in light of the paradigm of autonomous development exposes how dominant understandings of the American welfare and security state can create new hierarchies of domination and oppression that impede democratic citizenship. At the global level, autonomous development highlights the importance of constructing a world order based on collective self-determination understood as nondomination rather than in the usual narrow sense of freedom from external intervention. I conclude by considering ways in which the idea of autonomous development can be pushed further to better facilitate the practice of a feminist agenda of global empowerment.

Autonomous Development and Social Connection

The starting point for the paradigm of autonomous development is a relational understanding of agency.[2] Agency is relationally constituted when agents are not conceptualized as strictly separated from distinct others who neither influence them nor are influenced by them. In a relational conception, agents are always seen as embedded in multiple patterns of fluid social relations with others and autonomy refers to their ability to make their own decisions in a socially conscious manner. Social consciousness requires that agents recognize their relations with others and how their actions affect them. Autonomous decision making implies both the *prima facie* obligation of non-interference from others and the expectation that agents will be prepared to work together with others in common processes of adjudication, negotiation, and problem solving when the need arises. Such common processes may become necessary when conflicts or shared problems occur in social relations, or when agents' actions contribute to the emergence of problematic inequalities that perpetuate injustice.

Relational autonomy is closely tied to a commitment to promote justice in social relations, in light of the essential importance of a just social context for the autonomous development and exercise of agency. Justice, for Young, involves putting into place the institutional conditions for the elimination of oppression and domination.[3] Oppression occurs when agents are prevented from developing and exercising their individual capacities and possibilities for collective communication. Domination occurs when agents are inhibited from participation in determining their actions or the conditions for their actions. Both oppression and domination stand in the way of the autonomous development of agency. Both can present significant obstacles to the attainment of justice and democratic inclusion in a variety of social contexts, including global social relations. Finally, neither is intended as a comprehensive concept that encompasses all possible manifestations of unjust social relations – for example, Young acknowledges that her discussions of oppression and domination probably do not adequately address injustices that characterize peasant experiences – and both need to be contextually recast based on the concrete social relations under scrutiny.

The emphasis on eliminating oppression and domination from social relations leads to a concern with structural injustice.[4] The emphasis on structural analysis emerges from Young's acknowledgment of the structural inequalities that can pervade social institutions. Structural inequalities entail sets of reproduced social processes that reinforce one another to facilitate or constrain individual actions.[5] The problem with such entrenched processes is their tendency to reproduce social and economic inequalities in the political realm. In a context of structural inequality, members of groups who already possess social and economic advantages receive political advantages that facilitate their political actions, while members of disadvantaged groups find their political actions unfairly constrained. Broader group-based comparisons that reach beyond the political domain of formal equality are required for identifying and addressing structural inequality. Where structural social inequalities are widespread, democratic justice requires more than equal formal rights for representation and political participation; it also requires special measures for a better inclusion of the needs, interests, and perspectives of members of socially disadvantaged and marginalized groups in the political process in all relevant social contexts, domestic and global.[6]

The focus on structural injustice yields an account of political responsibility that moves beyond both personal responsibility and legal liability.[7] For Young, political responsibility has several features that make it particularly suitable for scrutinizing large-scale structural inequalities. Most significantly, unlike the legalistic liability model of responsibility with which it contrasts, political responsibility does not require the identification of a clear perpetrator for the harms suffered by a disadvantaged agent. Instead, it questions the normal operation of background conditions which structure relations between agents and give rise to reinforcing patterns of advantage and disadvantage.[8] As a result, unlike the liability model of responsibility, which focuses on reparations for harms suffered in the past, political responsibility is forward-looking and outcome-oriented, more open-ended about what constitutes its fulfilment, and more accommodating of schemes of shared responsibility. On this account, the expectations on the basis of which agents act in shared cooperative practices give rise to responsibilities that are shaped by and vary with the nature of the social context within which they interact. As Young summarizes: "all those who contribute by their actions to structural processes with some unjust outcomes share responsibility for the injustice" and have "an obligation to join with others who share that responsibility in order to transform the structural processes to make their outcomes less unjust."[9]

The paradigm of autonomous development brings these insights together. The relational conception of agency anchors autonomous development by positing agents who recognize their relations with and commitments to each other in making their decisions. The effective exercise of autonomous development requires the elimination of oppression and domination in social relations and, more broadly, the structural assessment of the justice of social institutions. Political responsibility emerges as key to the just stewarding of social relations favourable to autonomous development.

Social connection runs through all four aspects of autonomous development. Agents are conceived of as socially embedded and socially conscious from the start. Social justice and democratic inclusion are posited as essential for the autonomous development of agency in social contexts that are free from oppression and domination. Social institutions are evaluated in structural terms in order to ensure that pervasive patterns of social advantage and disadvantage are identified and addressed. Political responsibility is grounded in concrete social relations and aims to address the structural injustices that can arise from social embeddedness, both at home and abroad.

Autonomous Development and Democratic Citizenship

In democratic states, the paradigm of autonomous development requires putting into place conditions that facilitate the effective exercise of democratic values and political responsibility. In the specific context of the United States, democratic values are threatened by prominent versions of both the "welfare state" and "security state" paradigms, which Young criticizes for entrenching relations of domination and undermining the practice of democratic citizenship.

The welfare state paradigm, as it has been practiced in the United States, is problematic for Young because it establishes a hierarchy of domination between the providers and recipients of welfare. Welfare capitalism depoliticizes public life by placing distributive conflicts into the hands of presumably "impartial" experts and administrators.[10] The effect of privileging the false presumption of impartiality is the silencing of the perspectives of members of oppressed groups, who often tend to be the beneficiaries of welfare.[11] As a result, new forms of domination associated with the professionalized division of labour emerge, which further reinforce the distance between members of economically advantaged and disadvantaged groups. Welfare legislation is illustrative of the problematic practical implications of the welfare paradigm. Relying on an ideology of self-sufficiency through work, welfare policies are based on a discourse that reduces work to having a paid job, even if that job is exploitative and meaningless. Social contribution is erroneously equated with this impoverished notion of paid work in this ideology, and receiving social assistance is presented as a civic shortcoming. Thus, the practice of the welfare paradigm in the United States "systematically distorts people's understanding of their social conditions and reinforces unjust relations of economic and social power."[12]

The security state paradigm, as it has been practiced in the United States, is similarly problematic for Young because it establishes a hierarchy of domination between the providers and recipients of security. This hierarchy is best captured in the logic of masculinist protection, which is based in gendered relations of subordination.[13] In the masculinist protection bargain, women give up their autonomy in return for protection from aggression provided by the masculine head of the household. Men incur chivalrous self-sacrifices for the well-being of women, but only within this structure of familial subordination. Women who refuse to submit to the bargain face the possibility of aggression from other "bad" men and even attacks from their own supposed protectors. The gendered relations of domination that pervade the home are easily reproduced at the level of the state. Thus, the rulers of a security state conduct surveillance at home and wage war abroad, all in the name of protection. When citizens submit to arbitrary power and rulers rely on the mobilization of fear to justify their actions, democratic values suffer. Post–9/11 US politics illustrates the security bargain at work for Young, with wars in Afghanistan and Iraq being justified under the guise of protection and yielding an erosion of democratic rights and processes at home.

Both the welfare state and the security state paradigms undermine democratic citizenship, because they entrench hierarchies of domination that are inconsistent with autonomous development. Recipients of welfare are viewed as less than equal citizens in light of their inability to be self-sufficient without societal assistance. They are expected to submit to conditions set by already privileged and allegedly impartial experts – conditions that minimize their agency, fail to recognize their contributions to society, and deny them the possibility of seeking meaningful work. Recipients of security are expected to give up their autonomy and submit to the arbitrary decisions of their rulers, who freely mobilize fear and posit enemies to combat, at home and abroad. In both cases, relations of democratic equality are undermined, since the provided for and the protected are no longer equal to the providers and the protectors.

Rooted in a relational conception of agency, the autonomous development paradigm rejects both types of domination. Recognizing the social connections between autonomous agents, it calls for taking responsibility for the attainment of shared goals and the solution of shared problems within the framework of democratic political institutions that are based on mutual respect and political equality. Thus, Young emphasizes that the responsible provision of welfare and security begins from admitting that no state can ensure the welfare or guarantee the security of its citizens. Just like no individual is a self-sufficient and independent agent separate from others, no state can actually achieve full self-sufficiency and independence by itself in matters of welfare and security in an interconnected world. Neither should the state enact policies on the expectation that its citizens can realize these problematic ideals, in light of their adverse effects on autonomous development. The problem is multifaceted: policies that undermine the equality or rights of citizens are incompatible with democratic values; policies that make grand promises or offer guarantees must be regarded as generally suspect; and policies that are inattentive to existing patterns of oppression, domination, and structural injustice are inadequate. Instead, the attainment of welfare and security is largely a matter of carefully assessing the risks of and opportunities for action within webs of social relationships in light of their expected consequences and normative implications. Socially conscious cooperation with other implicated states and collectivities in order to tackle common problems and address broader structural injustices that affect welfare and security provision emerges as a key component of responsible democratic citizenship in this model.

Policies that extend the welfare and security paradigms to the world at large have to be replaced by policies that promote relations of mutual respect and political equality among the world's peoples. Citizens and rulers of wealthy and powerful states must not think they stand in a position of impartial paternal authority over the poorer and less powerful peoples and persons of the world simply because they have the capacity to provide or protect. Providers and protectors do not know what is best for their beneficiaries and must not make their assistance and rescue conditional upon terms that they set without the full participation of the provided for and protected.[14] Hierarchies of domination must be rejected by democratic citizens, both at home and abroad.

Autonomous Development and Global Democratic Justice

In global politics, the paradigm of autonomous development involves the establishment of just and democratic relations between self-determining collective units. Closely associated with democratic politics, collective self-determination has occupied an important normative place in twentieth-century international relations. Despite its normative appeal and widespread deployment in the process of decolonization, the meaning and scope of self-determination have been hotly contested. Consequently, in practice, the exercise of self-determination has generally been narrowly restricted to independence for former colonies, giving rise to an international system that has favoured the preservation of sovereignty in most other cases. The autonomous development paradigm questions the normative validity of sovereignty as it has traditionally been understood and posits collective self-determination as an essential building block of a just and democratic global order.

In fleshing out the contours of self-determination, Young compares her conception of "self-determination as non-domination" to the standard conception of "self-determination as non-intervention" associated with Westphalian sovereignty.[15] Self-determination as non-intervention involves exclusive control within a set of borders free from outside interference. For Young, this account of self-determination cannot adequately address the problem of domination for two reasons: first, many fluid relations of connection remain between newly independent colonies and former colonizers "the morning after sovereignty" in ways that enable ongoing relations of less formal external domination; and second, non-intervention does not protect persons and collectivities from new patterns of internal domination that may arise after independence.

Self-determination as nondomination does not falsely assume collectivities that are strictly separated from each other's webs of influence.

Neither does it bestow self-determining units with full and exclusive internal control and complete independence from external units. Being rooted in social connection and relational agency, self-determination as nondomination envisages socially embedded collectivities that make their decisions in socially conscious ways and are prepared to work with other collectivities when conflicts, common problems, or structural injustices occur. In ways that parallel the relational autonomy of individuals, self-determining entities set their own ends and act towards their realization, but within the limits of respect for and cooperation with other entities they interact with and are related to.

Despite Young's stark comparison, self-determination as nondomination does not need to stand in sharp opposition to self-determination as non-intervention. Instead, self-determination as nondomination can be understood to clarify the domain of application and limits of non-intervention. As in the case of individuals, self-determining collectivities can be thought to enjoy a *prima facie* presumption of external non-intervention, but within the limits of being attentive to the possible adverse effects their actions may have on others with whom they stand in a relation, which is a possibility that Young allows for.[16] Where serious relations of domination exist in external or internal relations, however, this *prima facie* presumption of non-intervention would be suspended. To address conflicts, common problems, and structural injustices that can emerge in their various relationships, self-determining entities would need to be ready to work together in shared democratic institutions they establish with other self-determining units on the basis of equal status and mutual respect.[17]

Despite paying extensive lip service to self-determination, the current international system does not enable its responsible practice. Westphalian sovereignty all too quickly associates self-determination with secession and strict non-intervention after independence for the collectivity exercising it, even though this does not adequately address the new forms of internal and external domination that may persist after sovereignty is attained. Furthermore, the international system does not adequately constrain power politics and aspirations for hegemonic domination. Hegemony is inherently prone to the pursuit of partial interests and can all too easily assume dictatorial forms, Young insists, even when it dresses itself up in benign motives such as the selfless promotion of the common good.[18] Dictatorship, for Young, refers to "a regime willing and able to exert its will without consulting with or answering to those affected by its decisions and actions."[19] Young describes the current hegemony of the United States in the international system as one of "aspiring dictatorship" because of its insistence "on demanding cooperation from other states on terms it sets" without consultation or adequate avenues for participation into its rule making, both in the economic and military realms.[20] Enforcement actions undertaken by the United States, as in the case of the war in Iraq or the vigorous pursuit of a narrowly supported Washington consensus in economic affairs, are illegitimate and must be countered by withdrawals of cooperation. Such foreign policy decisions are outward extensions of the security state and welfare state paradigms that must be rejected.

The realization of self-determination as nondomination requires moving beyond Westphalian sovereignty and hegemonic stability towards a pluralist international system with multilevel, democratic practices that can combine self-rule with shared rule.[21] Federal modes of governance can be particularly well suited for the institutionalization of these goals and can be crafted in a variety of ways to better correspond to the aspirations of the self-determining units working within them. While these units need not be territorially constituted, they need not exclude territorially constituted sovereign states, since states can be powerful self-determining collectivities.[22] Multiple levels of governance are necessary in Young's pluralist vision, but higher levels of governance do not necessarily have higher degrees of authority or decision-making power. The relationship between different levels ranging from local to regional to global is not one of centralization and hierarchy. Instead, each level is charged with functions that it can best accomplish in order to realize the overall goal of self-determination as nondomination and accountability flows in both directions. Lower-level units have autonomy within higher-level units in whose procedures and decisions they can participate. Higher-level units protect the autonomy of lower-level units within them, facilitate conflict resolution and cooperation among them, and attend to shared problems and structural concerns.

Global labour injustice and global economic inequalities offer prime examples of the structural concerns that would best be addressed at the global level in a multilevel, democratic international system. Young observes that serious harms are produced by structural processes that transcend state borders and configure global labour relations.[23] To illustrate, unhealthy working conditions and working relations replete with oppression and domination characterize sweatshops of the global apparel industry.[24] Located mostly in the global South, sweatshops supply apparel retailers who sell their goods mostly in the global North. Critical levels of need deprivation are widespread in many parts of the global South, which further constrain the autonomy of sweatshop workers, as well as the life and survival prospects of those who are not fortunate enough to have a sweatshop job. Background conditions that leave few options to individual workers are replayed at the level of collectivities when public authorities in developing countries compete with each other to attract global work orders by offering retail companies favourable cost-reducing bargains that come at the expense of workplace safety and labour justice.

These harmful structural processes cannot effectively be dealt with in a strictly state-centric international system and require multilevel governance mechanisms that can empower exploited workers. Forming sweatshop worker unions and involving them in decisions concerning workplace standards, ensuring representation from women in sweatshop governance schemes in an industry that employs mostly young women, joining global fair trade consumer movements that pressure apparel retailers to adopt and expect minimum workplace conditions from all their suppliers, devising intergovernmental cooperation mechanisms that create apparel taxes in the global North for goods manufactured in the global South and transfer these funds to public authorities in the countries of origin to reduce global economic inequalities are all possible examples of interrelated structural remedies for a structural problem that can be adopted in a democratic international system committed to autonomous development.

Practicing Autonomous Development

The paradigm of autonomous development inspired by Young has at least two important roles to play in the practice of a feminist agenda of global empowerment. The first role is interpretive and involves what Young calls ideology critique. Interpretation can expose problematic practices that stifle autonomous development. Interpretation reveals the hierarchies of domination that are embedded in prominent conceptions of welfare and security states, Westphalian sovereignty, hegemonic stability, and exploitative global labour practices. The second role is pragmatic and applies the main tenets and ideals of the autonomous development paradigm to concrete problems in democratic politics, comparative development, international relations, global ethics, and postcolonialism to devise better ways in which they may be addressed in a contextually sensitive manner. In both its interpretive and pragmatic moments, the paradigm of autonomous development takes gender seriously as an important dimension of analysis and aims to empower vulnerable agents caught in structurally unjust practices.[25]

Two areas of further investigation immediately become apparent for the practice of the interpretive and pragmatic roles of the paradigm of autonomous development. The first concerns the identification of concrete substantive principles that can specify the content of political responsibility in the context of particular cooperative practices. Here, the investigation runs into Young's general scepticism of the enterprise of specifying shared principles and can benefit from turning elsewhere. Somewhat surprisingly, Rawls, the grand theorist of principles of justice, emerges as a particularly useful conversation partner for this purpose.[26] Many points of connection exist between these two leading thinkers, as Young herself recognizes with respect to the significance they both attach to the basic structure of society for justice.[27] Interestingly, both thinkers are also explicitly critical of the institutions and practices of the United States, which they deem to be inadequately formal in justice terms. Echoing Young, Rawls is adamant about the essential importance of securing the fair value of political liberties to prevent domination. Examples of reforms Rawls favours to this end include publicly funded campaign financing, fair access to the media, and the progressive taxation of inheritance to prevent the accumulation of vast amounts of wealth and power in few hands over time.[28] Rawls also attaches great importance to assuring fair equality of opportunity for all citizens for the justice of the basic structure to be preserved, with important implications for many domains of life, including family laws that favour the full political inclusion of women as free and equal democratic citizens. Other themes in Rawls's work that accord the potential for a fruitful exchange include his commitment to pluralism, equality, and mutual respect in relations between peoples, all of which figure heavily in Young's vision for a pluralist and democratic international system.[29] In light of these affinities, a dialogue between Young and Rawls on justice may be mutually enriching, especially since the principles of justice that Rawls develops can fill in the gap that Young purposefully left in her work.

The second area of investigation is perhaps even more crucial for the practice of autonomous development. The paradigm of autonomous development is committed to enabling individuals to make their own choices about how to lead a meaningful life in a socially conscious

manner within institutional structures that prevent domination and oppression. Equal democratic citizenship at the domestic level and collective self-determination at the global level are posited as two important
·institutional avenues for the realization of autonomous development.
An important tension remains in this formulation between the autonomous development of individual persons and collective groups. This
tension calls for the continual balancing of the claims of individuals and
groups in particular contexts. To illustrate, how are the choices of individuals to leave their countries to be reconciled with the collective self-
determination of democratic states in matters of immigration? Aware of
potential clashes that could ensue between rival claims, Young charges
the global level of governance with the task of protecting individuals
inside self-determining units from severe rights violations.[30] A lot more
needs to be said about what rights individuals have in which contexts
and for what reason before this vision of global governance can be
meaningfully institutionalized. There is the added question of whether
the global level is indeed the most appropriate place for resolving ten-
sions over individual rights that arise in lower-level self-determining
entities. According these powers to the global level seems to privilege
higher levels of governance in ways that Young is not generally prepared to do and can undermine the two-way flow of accountability
between levels. Federalism in itself does not (and should not) provide
a clear-cut solution, since the specific balances of power and authority that are negotiated in federal systems can vary greatly. Ultimately,
the ever-present tension between the autonomous development of individual persons and the autonomous development of a multiplicity of
competing (and perhaps even overlapping) collectivities offers another
strong invitation for the elaboration of contextually sensitive substantive principles that can guide the adjudication of competing claims in
ways that promote global empowerment.

NOTES

1 Some of these essays were reprinted in Iris Marion Young, *Global Chal-
   lenges: War, Self-determination, and Responsibility for Justice* (Cambridge:
   Polity, 2007).
2 Iris Marion Young, *Inclusion and Democracy* (Oxford: Oxford University
   Press, 2000); Young, "Two Concepts of Self-determination," in *Human
   Rights: Concepts, Contests, Contingencies*, ed. Austin Sarat and Thomas

R. Kearns (Michigan: University of Michigan Press, 2001), 25–44; Young, "Modest Reflections on Hegemony and Global Democracy," *Theoria: A Journal of Social and Political Theory*, no. 103 (April 2004): 1–14; and Young, "Self-determination as Non-domination: Ideals Applied to Palestine/Israel," *Ethnicities* 5, no. 2 (2005): 139–59, http://dx.doi. org/10.1177/1468796805052112.

3 Iris Marion Young, *Justice and the Politics of Difference* (Princeton, NJ: Princeton University Press, 1990).

4 Young, *Justice and the Politics of Difference*; Young, *Inclusion and Democracy*; Young, "Equality of Whom? Social Groups and Judgments of Injustice," *Journal of Political Philosophy* 9, no. 1 (2001): 1–18, http://dx.doi. org/10.1111/1467-9760.00115; and Young, "Modest Reflections."

5 Young, *Inclusion and Democracy*, and Young, "Two Concepts of Self-determination."

6 In her recognition of the necessity of group-based comparisons and group-specific measures to attain democratic justice, Young echoes many of the concerns of the group-based representation literature. Young, *Justice and the Politics of Difference*, and Young, *Inclusion and Democracy*. For prominent examples of proponents of group-based representation, see Will Kymlicka, *Multicultural Citizenship: A Liberal Theory of Minority Rights* (Oxford: Clarendon, 1995); Anne Phillips, *The Politics of Presence* (Oxford: Clarendon, 1995); Michael Saward, ed., *Democratic Innovation: Deliberation, Representation, and Association* (New York: Routledge, 2000); and Melissa Williams, *Voice, Trust, and Memory: Marginalized Groups and the Failings of Liberal Representation* (Princeton, NJ: Princeton University Press, 1998).

7 Iris Marion Young, "Responsibility and Global Labor Justice," *Journal of Political Philosophy* 12, no. 4 (2004): 365–88, http://dx.doi.org/10.1111/j.1467-9760.2004.00205.x; Young, "Responsibility and Global Justice: A Social Connection Model," *Social Philosophy & Policy* 23, no. 1 (2006): 102–30, http://dx.doi.org/10.1017/S0265052506060043; and Young, *Responsibility for Justice* (New York: Oxford University Press, 2011), http://dx.doi. org/10.1093/acprof:oso/9780195392388.001.0001. Young calls this the social connection model of political responsibility. I purposefully use the name "political responsibility" instead of "the social connection model" to not give the misleading impression that social connection is important only for responsibility. Instead, social connection is the essential starting point for all four dimensions of autonomous development.

8 For a concrete application of the political responsibility model to the case of Hurricane Katrina, see Iris Marion Young, "Katrina: Too Much Blame,

Not Enough Responsibility," *Dissent* 53, no. 1 (2006): 41–6, http://dx.doi.org/10.1353/dss.2006.0052.

9 Young, *Responsibility for Justice*, 96.

10 Young, *Justice and the Politics of Difference*.

11 Young emphasized that the presumption of impartiality was false because there can be no real impartiality. All perspectives always come from some place to which they are partial. Young, *Justice and the Politics of Difference*.

12 Iris Marion Young, "New Disciplines of Work and Welfare," *Dissent* 47, no. 3 (2000): 26.

13 Iris Marion Young, "Feminist Reactions to the Contemporary Security Regime," *Hypatia* 18, no. 1 (2003): 223–31, http://dx.doi.org/10.1111/j.1527-2001.2003.tb00792.x, and Young, "The Logic of Masculinist Protection: Reflections on the Current Security State," *Signs* 29, no. 1 (2003): 1–25, http://dx.doi.org/10.1086/375708.

14 Young, "Logic of Masculinist Protection."

15 Young, *Inclusion and Democracy*; Young, "Two Concepts of Self-determination"; Young, "Self-determination and Global Democracy: A Critique of Liberal Nationalism," in *Multiculturalism in Contemporary Societies: Perspectives on Difference and Transdifference*, ed. Helmbrecht Breinig, Jürgen Gebhardt, and Klaus Lösch (Erlangen: Universitätsbund Erlangen-Nürnberg, 2002), 91–123; and Young, "Self-determination as Non-domination."

16 Young, "Self-determination as Non-domination."

17 Ibid.

18 Young, "Modest Reflections."

19 Young, *Global Challenges*, 146.

20 Ibid.

21 Young, "Modest Reflections."

22 Young herself tends to be more critical of territorially organized federal units than I am presenting here, but I believe this is because of her scepticism of the widespread association of territorially organized states with the main (and perhaps only) possible realization of federalism.

23 Iris Marion Young, "From Guilt to Solidarity: Sweatshops and Political Responsibility," *Dissent* 50, no. 2 (2003): 39–44.

24 Young, "Responsibility and Global Labor Justice," and Young, "Responsibility and Global Justice."

25 Iris Marion Young, "Lived Body vs. Gender: Reflections on Social Structure and Subjectivity," *Ratio: An International Journal of Analytic Philosophy* 15, no. 4 (2002): 410–28.

26 John Rawls, *A Theory of Justice* (Cambridge, MA: Harvard University Press, 1971); John Rawls, *Political Liberalism* (New York: Columbia University Press, 1996); John Rawls, *Collected Papers* (Cambridge, MA: Harvard University Press, 1999); John Rawls, *The Law of Peoples* (Cambridge, MA: Harvard University Press, 1999); and John Rawls, *Justice as Fairness: A Restatement* (Cambridge, MA: Harvard University Press, 2001).
27 Iris Marion Young, "Taking the Basic Structure Seriously," *Perspectives on Politics* 4, no. 1 (2006): 91–7, http://dx.doi.org/10.1017/S1537592706060099.
28 Rawls, *Justice as Fairness.*
29 Rawls, *Law of Peoples.*
30 Young, *Global Challenges*, 150.

5   Political Responsibility for Decolonization in Canada[1]

MELISSA S. WILLIAMS

Introduction

Theoretical models of political responsibility, including those articulated by Iris Marion Young, offer helpful insights into a range of pressing questions of justice. The issue I consider here is decolonization. Questions of decolonization in Canada are illuminated by models of political responsibility, but they also reveal some of the limitations of these models.

Conceptions of political responsibility can help to clarify, if not wholly resolve, who should take responsibility for which dimensions of the complex project of decolonization. At the same time, there is no one single model of political responsibility that will make sense of the whole picture of responsibility for decolonization. Instead, different models of responsibility highlight different agents in different structures of relationship. Any attempt to reduce the concept of political responsibility for decolonization to a single model occludes other structures of responsibility that are equally relevant and necessary to achieve justice. When it comes to the politics surrounding decolonization, this is a dangerous phenomenon. The exclusive focus on a single model or structure of political responsibility will enable actors validly to claim that they are taking responsibility even when their doing so is far from adequate. Such was the danger, I believe, with the 2008 apology for Native residential schools by Canada's prime minister Stephen Harper. It constituted a genuine and important act of political responsibility taking, but was nonetheless only a fragment of the responsibility that must be shouldered by various actors (including but not only the Canadian state) if decolonization is ever to be complete.

In this chapter, following a brief outline of the history of colonialism in Canada, I offer a settler perspective on political responsibility for decolonization by examining four models of responsibility: fiduciary, liability, social contract, and social connection. I argue that although Iris Young's social connection model offers rich resources for conceptualizing political responsibility for decolonization in Canada, each of the other models adds to our understanding of the respective responsibilities of different kinds of social and political agents. In the final analysis, we need a pluralistic account of political responsibility in order to identify the distinct structural opportunities confronting the varied actors who jointly share moral responsibility for the vast and complex project of decolonization.

Colonialism and the Contemporary Canadian Context

On June 11, 2008, Canadian prime minister Stephen Harper stood up in the House of Commons and delivered a formal apology to Indigenous people who suffered the government's century-long policy of forcibly removing Indigenous children from their families and communities and placing them in residential schools run predominantly by the Catholic, Anglican, United, and Presbyterian churches. Acknowledging that the policy was directly aimed at assimilating Indigenous children into the dominant culture, and affirming that assimilationist policy is wrong, Harper stated,

> The government now recognizes that the consequences of the Indian residential schools policy were profoundly negative and that this policy has had a lasting and damaging impact on aboriginal culture, heritage and language.
> While some former students have spoken positively about their experiences at residential schools – these stories are far overshadowed by tragic accounts of the emotional, physical, and sexual abuse and neglect of helpless children and their separation from powerless families and communities. The legacy of Indian residential schools has contributed to social problems that continue to exist in many communities today.
> It has taken extraordinary courage for the thousands of survivors that have come forward to speak publicly about the abuse they suffered.
> ...
> The government recognizes that the absence of an apology has been an impediment to healing and reconciliation. Therefore, on behalf of the

government of Canada and all Canadians, I stand before you, in this chamber so central to our life as a country, to apologize to aboriginal peoples for Canada's role in the Indian residential schools system.[2]

The apology was a powerful moment in Canadian history.[3] It acknowledged the wrongfulness of the residential schools policy and the extreme harm caused by the policy to its immediate victims and to their children, families, and communities, and it validated the Indigenous experience of residential schools as an injustice whose enormity is beyond measurement. It was deeply respectful of Indigenous communities in its language, tone, and content. Symbolically, it mattered that the apology was delivered by the prime minister in the very House of Commons that legislated the policy. It mattered that the apology was affirmed and expressed by the leader of every major party. It mattered that Indigenous leaders and residential school survivors from First Nations, Inuit, Métis, and urban Indigenous communities were present in the House and had an opportunity to respond. For many residential school survivors and their families, this official, public, and apparently sincere apology for the harms they suffered was a signal turning point in their own process of coping with the trauma inflicted by residential schools and echoed in the resulting family and social dysfunction in so many Native communities.

It also mattered that the apology itself, though generated by the same political and legal forces that produced the Indian Residential Schools Settlement Agreement, went beyond the legal obligations of the government of Canada. This voluntary embrace of moral and political responsibility for public wrongs supports at least a glimmer of hope that non-Indigenous Canadians take seriously a moral obligation to put their relationship with Indigenous peoples on a better footing and to take responsibility for the future well-being of Indigenous communities. This hope also surrounds the Truth and Reconciliation Commission created as part of the Settlement Agreement.

At its most promising, then, the apology appeared to signal a sincere will to take responsibility for decolonizing settler-Indigenous relationships in Canada. Further encouragement could be drawn from public opinion research conducted at the behest of the Truth and Reconciliation Commission, which suggested that the will to take responsibility for repairing the relationship is widely shared among Canadians.[4]

But critics of the apology and the TRC process cautioned against hopes that the apology signalled a new, decolonizing phase of Canada's history, with good reason. Although an increasing number of First Nations communities have developed innovative economies and robust institutions of public service provision and governance, Indigenous people are still the most disadvantaged social group in Canada.[5] Child poverty, poor housing, poor education, overrepresentation in prisons, and low labour market participation continue to characterize both on-reserve and off-reserve Indigenous populations.[6] Many reserves lack potable drinking water. Health problems and suicide rates are much higher among Indigenous people than in the general population. Violence against Indigenous women continues at epidemic rates.[7] Land claims against federal and provincial governments continue to drag on after decades of unsuccessful negotiation.

The persistent and dramatic gap between the well-being of Indigenous people and settler Canadians is partial evidence of an ongoing relationship of colonialism.[8] For most scholars of Indigenous peoples in Canada, these ongoing patterns of inequality are unmistakably linked to historic patterns of the dispossession of lands and the deliberate destruction of Indigenous cultures, languages, and life ways – all classic features of settler colonialism. Equally clear is the historic pattern of *political* dispossession through which Indigenous peoples have been subjected to alien orders of law and deprived of their powers of self-determination.[9] In particular, the Indian Act structures through which the federal government relates to Indigenous peoples continue to embody a deeply colonial project of state control over their land, membership, economies, and political institutions. It is beyond the scope of this chapter to offer a systematic analytic account of the defining features of colonial power, which would be necessary for a full defence of this claim. As Frances Abele has argued in detail, however, key features of the Indian Act run contrary to the standards of political legitimacy that are fundamental to western democratic orders, and place First Nations communities in a relationship of subordination to and control by the Canadian state. These include: the title and political authority of the federal government over First Nations reserve lands and resources (to be managed in accordance with principles of fiduciary responsibility for which the government is not accountable to the community);[10] the unilateral definition of the political process by which band councils are elected; the power to regulate the minutiae of band council governance, including council meeting dates, presiding officers, public notice of meetings, etc.; the requirement that band councils report all their decisions to the minister of Indian affairs; the definition and regulation of band membership; the power to invalidate the sale of agricultural products by band members to non-band members; the empowerment of other levels of government to expropriate reserve lands, with the consent of the federal government but without the consent of the band; the power to determine the use of band monies (with band consent); and so on. As Abele concludes,

> The people who live under the Indian Act in Canada live in unique circumstances. There are no other citizens of Canada for whom a specific piece of federal legislation regulates their social and political citizenship, and the most fundamental features of their social and economic lives. No other groups of people, except those who are in prisons, live so thoroughly under the supervision and control of the executive branch of the federal government.[11]

No Indigenous person is likely to disagree with the claim that governments, including band council governments, have a responsibility for the delivery of effective programs and policies in accordance with sound fiscal management, and should be held accountable for their exercise of power and their use of public funds. But democratic principles of political legitimacy require that accountability for good governance is owed to those who live *under* a political authority. Indian Act structures direct the accountability of band councils upward, to the federal government, and this structure overwhelms and supersedes their accountability to the members of the communities they are meant to serve. To the extent Indian Act structures do provide for direct accountability to band members, they require conformity to electoral and decision-making institutions which are pale reflections of western notions of democratic legitimacy and were imposed upon Indigenous peoples by the federal government rather than designed and chosen by themselves. Thus, for many Indigenous people, the task of overcoming colonialism includes, crucially, the development of alternatives to Indian Act governance structures that are grounded in their own historical practices of governance and the constructions of legitimacy, authorization, and accountability that were embedded in those practices. There is a wave of new constitution making in Indigenous communities across Canada, developing innovative institutions of self-government to replace the Indian Act, enable self-defined strategies of economic development, and replace accountability to the federal government with accountability to their own people according to their own standards.[12]

The foregoing is a very rough sketch of the state of colonialism and decolonization in contemporary Canada, which doubtless omits elements that others will view as central. As such, it leaves very open the question of how we should understand the key characteristics of both colonialism and decolonization, though by drawing on some of the most commonly noted features of Indigenous peoples' relationship to the Canadian state, it offers some hints. A relationship of settler colonialism, we might infer, is one in which, *inter alia*,

- the economic benefits of the land and other natural resources flow disproportionately to the settler population as compared with the Indigenous population, and the disposition of these resources is largely decided by a state that is not effectively accountable to Indigenous people (we might call this economic colonialism);[13]
- the well-being and opportunities for human flourishing of the colonized are less than those of the population to whom authorities are politically accountable;
- the colonized are characterized as morally, culturally, mentally, or developmentally deficient, and this is used as a justification for the control of their land and resources by the state;
- the colonized lack effective means of political control over those who have coercive power over them;[14] Indigenous people are deprived of the powers of self-government through institutions that they regard as legitimate, according to standards of legitimacy that make sense to them from within their own cultural frameworks (taken together, we might call these features political colonialism).

Correlatively, decolonization seems to entail one or more of the following:

- restoring to the colonized population the benefit of the land and resources that it rightfully has claim to;
- dismantling the laws, stereotypes, and norms by which people are stigmatized as morally inferior, and through which they are deprived of agency over their own lives, and addressing the trauma suffered as a consequence of that stigmatization;
- redistributing resources and opportunities so that members of the formerly colonized population have life chances that are no worse than those of the settler population (including the chance of sharing family and intergenerational community as sources of healthy individual development);
- establishing institutions that secure legitimating political authorization and accountability to the people from those who exercise

decision-making power over their life circumstances, according to standards of legitimacy that make sense to them on their own cultural terms.

Let us suppose that colonialism, understood in this rather rough sense, is an injustice (or perhaps rather a bundle or syndrome of injustices), and therefore that decolonization is a duty of justice. As a guide to practice, this is rather unhelpful, for it does not tell us very much about who bears what sort of responsibility for bringing about decolonization. That is the question to which I now turn.

Models of Political Responsibility

The Fiduciary Model

I begin with a model of political responsibility that is not included in Young's typology, but which looms large in the context of Canadian colonialism. Since the Royal Proclamation of 1763, the Crown's fiduciary responsibility towards Indigenous peoples has been the fulcrum of its constitutional and legal obligations to respect Indigenous rights.[15] The Royal Proclamation states,

> [I]t is just and reasonable, and essential to our Interest, and the Security of our Colonies, that the several Nations or Tribes of Indians with whom We are connected, and *who live under our Protection*, should not be molested or disturbed in the Possession of such Parts of Our Dominions and Territories as, not having been ceded to or purchased by Us, are reserved to them, or any of them, as their Hunting Grounds.[16]

The concept of fiduciary responsibility – etymologically derived from the Latin *fides*, meaning trust, faith, fidelity – expresses a relationship of trusteeship in which the trustee has power or control over resources which he or she is obligated to exercise in the interests of the other party. Fiduciary responsibility in Crown-Indigenous relations has been the major instrument for legitimating colonial power; it was certainly key in the justification and rationale for the residential schools policy, as in other examples of the *mission civilatrice* of European colonialism. We might therefore think that a model of fiduciary responsibility on the part of the state can have no place in a decolonizing process.

But this would be an overhasty conclusion, I believe. First, the Crown's fiduciary responsibility towards Indigenous peoples has constitutional status and has been interpreted as a *sui generis* obligation – that is to say, the Crown's duties to Indigenous people are not comparable to its duties towards any other actor.[17] In the law, the "honour of the Crown" is at stake in meeting its fiduciary responsibilities, giving them a constitutional weight which, from a strategic point of view, it might be imprudent for Indigenous peoples to relinquish.

Beyond the strategic consideration, however, some notion of fiduciary responsibility is inherent in the modern concept of state sovereignty. Though we may wish to move beyond a political order structured by the system of sovereign states towards an order of dispersed power and authority,[18] there is no getting around the fact that the territorial sovereign state remains the dominant political-legal structure of the contemporary world.

As long as we have such states, their fiduciary responsibility for the basic well-being of their populations is the *sine qua non* of political legitimacy; at least since Hobbes, it is the core justification for the concentration of power in the sovereign. The state's fiduciary responsibility towards its population is what makes sense of the concept of the failed state that looms large in contemporary justifications for external intervention, as when people invoke an international "responsibility to protect" victims of gross human rights violations. It is what makes sense of claims for the state's duty to rescue its people in times of emergency, including natural disasters. It is what gives weight to the charge that it should be a source of shame for wealthy modern societies when their people are living in "Third World" conditions, a charge levelled against Canada in critiques of the abysmal conditions on northern reserves and the United States during the Hurricane Katrina disaster. A fuller account of the centrality of fiduciary responsibility to the concept of modern state sovereignty would take us to Foucault's analysis of the rise of the *Polizeistaat* as a regime of household management charged with looking after and managing the biological needs of people conceived as a *population* living within a *territory* – all concepts that are highly relevant to understanding the Canadian state's relationship with Indigenous people.

As the nod to Foucault implies, one important thing to note about the model of state fiduciary responsibility is that it allows no theoretical space for the political agency of the governed; all of the agency in this model lies with the state. Those who live under the power of the state are entitled to its protection, but they are passive subjects, not active citizens. It is a model of political responsibility that is defined through and through by state paternalism, which is abundantly clear in the language of the Royal Proclamation ("Our loving Subjects") itself. For this reason, the fiduciary model of political responsibility is wholly compatible with what I've called "political colonialism," the deprivation of powers of self-rule by Indigenous peoples.

But it still bears some potential importance in a process of decolonization because it is incompatible with what I've tagged as "economic colonialism," the exploitation of colonized people's land, resources, and (relatively rarely in settler colonialism) labour for the benefit of the colonizer and to the detriment of the colonized.[19] The state is in clear violation of its fiduciary responsibility when it separates people from the means of their economic survival, exposes them to disease, or fails to provide adequately for the basic conditions of existence (housing, medical care, education, water). As suggested earlier, the ongoing circumstances of so many Indigenous communities are therefore an indictment of the Canadian state for its utter failure in meeting its claimed fiduciary responsibilities towards Indigenous peoples. The harm caused through residential schools was also a deep failure of fiduciary responsibility, which is why an official state apology and reparations were so fitting and necessary as an element of decolonization.

As the Royal Proclamation highlights, the state's fiduciary responsibility also provides a strong rationale for the exercise of state power against third-party colonialism, the economic exploitation or human rights violations of Indigenous people by nonstate actors such as corporations, churches, or individuals. Still, there might appear to be some tension between claiming an ongoing fiduciary responsibility of the Canadian state towards Indigenous peoples and a process of political decolonization, in which the powers of state sovereignty and jurisdiction over broad areas of public policy are recovered by self-governing Indigenous communities. If self-determination entails that Indigenous governments assume their own fiduciary responsibilities towards their people's basic needs, then does it mean that Indigenous communities abandon their claim to the protection of the Canadian state?

The answer is clearly no. The process of colonialism systematically deprives Indigenous peoples of both the economic and political capacities to provide for their communities' basic needs and security, and the

Canadian state cannot abandon its fiduciary obligations at the limit – where Indigenous governments have not yet recovered that capacity, the state must provide a backstop on an interim basis, working in the meantime to support Indigenous governments in building their own state-like capacities. Further, few envision that Indigenous governments will ever take on the full features of the modern territorial sovereign state, or see that as a desirable objective. Rather, the most promising models for decolonization envision a diffusion and sharing of the powers associated with the sovereign state across multiple governmental actors – not unlike the parcelling out of sovereignty that international relations theorists see as the direction we should be (and are) taking in reshaping a globalizing world regulated by an order of international law. Decolonization is consistent with this unbundling and redistribution of states' fiduciary responsibility across a range of accountable political governments.

The Liability Model

In discussing the liability model of responsibility, I will simply follow Young. This model holds people morally or legally responsible for the harmful consequences of their actions when there is a specific and identifiable causal connection between their actions and those consequences. Liability requires that the responsible agent performed the harmful actions voluntarily and "with adequate knowledge of the situation."[20] The model is applicable to both individual and collective agents.

It is worth noticing that the language of liability is often highly legalized; it is difficult to bootstrap a model of responsibility-as-liability outside an established legal order. Since holding people liable for the harms caused by their actions entails either punishment or other forms of retribution, it requires some form of organized power to mete out the penalties. More importantly, it is normally through the categories of wrong recognized and established in law that people are held responsible for their harmful actions. At the height of colonial domination, this means that a liability model of responsibility for harm to colonized people is unlikely to be very useful, since the legal orders of colonial regimes are unlikely to recognize harms to colonized peoples as wrongs. This is a subcategory of the more general problem of the rule of law in wicked regimes.

But in transitional contexts – where a wicked regime gives way to a more just (or less wicked) one – the liability model has an important role to play, even if this role is problematic from the standpoint of theories of the rule of law. From the Nuremburg trials to truth and reconciliation commissions in South Africa and elsewhere, liability for human rights violations that were not recognized as crimes in the preceding legal order has been understood as a crucial instrument in the project of breaking with the unjust past and moving forward to a more just future. In nontransitional contexts, too (i.e., stable democracies such as Canada and the United States), apologies and reparations for the past wrongs of the state have been understood as a way to acknowledge *as wrongs* actions that caused great harm, even if they were not technically illegal, and thereby to lay a foundation for reconstituting political community on a more just basis.[21]

In Canada, apologies and reparations for (to take two prominent examples) the Chinese Head Tax and Japanese-Canadian internment during World War II both were designed to achieve the purpose of generating a sense of full membership in Canadian society among classes of citizens who had been wronged. The Indian Residential Schools Settlement Agreement similarly seeks to establish the equal status of Indigenous persons and non-Indigenous citizens as moral claimants against the state and other social agents.

The liability model of responsibility, then, has an important role to play in decolonization. Although it is seldom likely to yield complete restitution for harms to Indigenous people, each successful use of it further undermines the colonial order's premise that dominating the natives is justified by their lesser moral worth. When nonstate actors are held liable for their role in human rights violations, as with the churches in the residential schools cases and settlement, the liability model also sends a clear warning to civil society actors that they will be held responsible for their actions with respect to Indigenous people – an important corrective to colonial regimes in which settlers were not prosecuted for the harms they caused to natives.

The centrepiece of Young's critique of the liability model (and the springboard for turning to alternative models of political responsibility) is that it "relies on a fairly direct interaction between the wrongdoer and the wronged party."[22] Consequently, while it is a necessary instrument of justice, it is insufficient in cases where harms are caused by complex systems of interaction rather than by specific identifiable agents. Indeed, she argues, in structures of domination it may often be the case that "those with the greatest power ... or those who derive benefits ... may well be removed from any interaction with those who

are most harmed."[23] Making sense of intuitions about moral and political responsibility for more diffuse structures of injustice requires a
different model of moral-political relationship than the narrow agent-
victim relationship envisioned in the liability model. Responsibility-
as-liability is a necessary feature of political-legal order in a just society,
but it is not sufficient because it does not enable us to identify or respond to wider patterns of unjust power hierarchy. The social contract
tradition and Young's social connection model of political responsibility offer more expansive views.

The Social Contract Model

The basic idea of a social contract is that human beings live in social
relationship with one another, and this relationship generates mutual
obligation. This obligation is formalized and specified by a social contract in which parties agree to the terms of living together and form
a political community. That political community constitutes a government which serves as the instrument through which its members meet
their obligations towards one another and secure their own protection.
Membership in such a political community generates responsibilities
for both individual citizens and government. Government has the responsibility to protect the rights and interests of citizens and to fairly
distribute the benefits and burdens of cooperation. Individual members have a responsibility to carry their fair share of the burdens of social cooperation (through taxation, compliance with valid laws, respect
for one another's rights, etc.), and to hold government responsible for
performing its duties (through the exercise of political rights).

As Rawls's *A Theory of Justice* makes explicit, the social contract model
of political responsibility establishes two different types of obligation
among citizen-members. The first is that of constitutional fundamen-
tals, spelling out the basic rights and duties of each member of political
society. One might think of these as the perfect duties (in the Kantian
sense) that attach to membership in a formally constituted political
order. The second type of responsibility is more general and open-
ended; one might think of these responsibilities as imperfect duties in
the Kantian sense, responsibilities that are not specifiable in advance
and are generated by the unpredictable contingencies of human living-
together. It is this sense of responsibility that I believe Rawls intends to
invoke when he writes of the social contract as an agreement "to share
one another's fate."[24] It entails a generalized responsibility to conduct

political and social arrangements so as to share the contingent benefits and burdens of living-together on terms that are reciprocal and aimed at mutual advantage over the long term.[25]

The context of settler colonialism, such as exists in Canada, adds a further layer of complexity to the array of responsibilities that generate from a social contract model. To have a claim to legitimacy, settler colonialism depends upon the consent of the prior occupants of the land to share that land with newcomers. As made explicit in the Royal Proclamation of 1763, treaties between the Crown and the Indigenous inhabitants of the land constitute the compact that renders settler's presence, their use of the land and its resources, legitimate.[26] Treaties, then, constitute a second level of social contract between *collectivities*: the settler society taken as a whole, represented by the Crown; and Indigenous societies, represented by the leaders they have authorized to conclude treaties on their behalf. The idea that the fundamental legitimacy of settler society in Canada rests upon explicit treaty relationships runs deep in Indigenous peoples' view that their relationship with Canada is a nation-to-nation relationship, and not a subjection to the sovereignty of the Crown. It is expressed clearly and eloquently in the Gus-Wen-Tah or Two-Row Wampum that is often invoked as a model of a just relationship between Indigenous peoples and Canada.[27] It makes sense to think of treaties as *social* contracts, and not just contracts *simpliciter*, because they are agreements to remain in relationship *into the distant future* rather than time-limited agreements for a narrowly specified exchange of benefits. The long time-horizon of these relationships warrants understanding them as *relationships of political community* and not narrow contracts.

Treaty-based relationship, understood as a social contract between Indigenous and settler communities, can also be understood as generating two types of political responsibility analogous to those generated by the individual-level social contract. The first type, corresponding to what I have characterized as the perfect duties that flow from the contract, is constituted by the express commitments made by the Crown and particular Indigenous peoples in the negotiation of the contract agreement: in most cases, the commitment by the Crown to transfer material resources to the Indigenous community in exchange for the use of specified tracts of the people's traditional lands. The second type, corresponding to what I have called the imperfect duties that attach to membership in a social contract, is constituted by a generalized commitment between the parties to cooperate on terms of mutual advantage on a long time-horizon. Here, the responsibility is a more generalized, contingent, and non-specific one to act in the interests of the other party in such a way as to warrant an ongoing relationship of trust. Acting on this duty requires attentiveness to the particular circumstances in which an agent finds herself, being mindful of specific opportunities to support political measures, initiate public actions, or participate in public debates so as to contribute to broader processes of decolonization. Such actions might be small, as when one intervenes in a conversation in which others are repeating worn stereotypes about Indigenous people. They might be moderate in scale, as in participating in a public demonstration in support of Indigenous rights. Or they might be major, such as taking a leadership role in efforts to change state policy, in social movements aimed at shifting public consciousness about Indigenous issues, or in efforts to revive and institutionalize the teaching of Indigenous languages. How individuals perform the imperfect duty of decolonizing Canadian society will vary according to their skills, social positions, and unpredictable opportunities to make a difference.

There is a connection – and some potential contradiction – between the fiduciary obligations of the Crown towards Indigenous peoples and the treaty-based conception of a social contract.[28] Although space does not permit me to explore the point in much depth, it may be that the Crown's fiduciary responsibility lies within this second type of responsibility, and is characterized by a general obligation not to act in a manner contrary to the interests of Indigenous communities and, at the limit, to make use of its powers and resources[29] to protect its treaty partners from serious harm if their powers to protect themselves are insufficient. So understood, this trust-based responsibility is reciprocal, so that in the event an Indigenous community's land or resources were needed to provide protection, at the limit, for the most basic needs of settler society, it would also make use of those resources to come to the aid of settlers. I imagine it is not difficult to find ample historical examples of moments when Indigenous communities did in fact provide such aid to treaty partners. The intuition is that the responsibility to provide aid and protection to treaty partners with whom one has a relationship of long standing and extending into a distant future is stronger than the duty to provide aid to distant others.

If we accept this two-level (individual and collective) and two-type (perfect and imperfect, or specific and generalized) account of the responsibilities that are rendered coherent by a social contract model, then what follows for our understanding of responsibilities for decolonization? First, it is useful to make clear who the agents of responsibility are in this model. They are: (1) individuals within the social contracts that constitute (a) Canada (itself a confederation which includes provincial political communities that may also be understood in social contract terms) and (b) Indigenous peoples as political communities; and (2) the governments of Canada and of Indigenous treaty partners.

The dimensions of decolonization that seem especially pertinent from a social contract perspective are those that connect to the treaty relationship between Canada and Indigenous peoples. If, as suggested at the end of the first section, colonial domination consists importantly in depriving Indigenous peoples of the use of the lands and resources that they traditionally enjoyed, without their consent, then the treaty dimension of a social contract model of responsibility yields an understanding of decolonization as the restoration of land and resources on terms that they can now consent to – or did consent to in past treaties, so many of which have been violated by the Canadian state. This idea underscores the importance of the government of Canada's responsibility to conclude the negotiation of pending land claims and treaties in an expeditious manner, as has been acknowledged by the federal government and is being especially vigorously pursued by the government of British Columbia.

But beyond this, the treaty-based social contract model entails a responsibility of settler-citizens of Canada and the provinces to acknowledge that they, too, are treaty-governed people, and that their right to enjoy the benefits of the land they occupy is conditioned on ongoing treaty-based obligations to provide material compensation to Indigenous peoples for the use of the land. Thus, a major responsibility of both Canadian governments and citizens is to acknowledge that transfer payments from the federal government to Indigenous communities are not a form of welfare or handout, but are compensation for the loss of the forms of political economy through which they sustained themselves historically – forms of political economy that required, in many cases, that they maintain patterns of seasonal migration over fairly large territories. In the idealized treaty-based view of relationship with the Crown, Indigenous peoples accepted material goods in compensation for the loss of their traditional economic livelihood when they resettled on much more restrictive territories. Such settlement was never understood by them to entail the relinquishment of the seasonal patterns of hunting and harvest that were essential to their survival.

It is also central to the treaty-based view that Indigenous peoples never lost title to their lands or their right to rule themselves. These rights were acknowledged in the Supreme Court of Canada's decision in the *Delgamuukw* case.[30]

In short, re-educating settler-citizens that they are major beneficiaries of Canada's treaty relationships with Indigenous peoples is a central task of decolonization. Both citizens and the government bear responsibility for accomplishing this re-education. Arguably, we should understand this responsibility as among the perfect duties that flow from the social contract model.

The Social Connection Model

Young develops her social connection model of political responsibility in order to argue against two different camps in political theory: those who argue that we have duties of justice only towards members of our own political communities (her focus is on David Miller), and cosmopolitans who argue that we owe equal duties of justice to all human beings as such. The first is too narrow an account of responsibility, she argues, and the latter is too large. Her social connection model argues that connection to others through social structures does matter, but that we need not understand shared membership in a political community as the only social structure that is relevant from the standpoint of responsibility for justice.

The social connection model rests centrally on Young's view that injustice results not only from the conscious actions of specifiable agents but also from complex systems of interaction whose adverse effects are neither intended nor even perceived by the agents who are operating within them. Structural injustice, she states,

> exists when social processes put large categories of persons under systematic threat of domination or *deprivation of the means to develop and exercise their capacities*, at the same time as these processes enable others to dominate or have a wide range of opportunities for developing and exercising their capacities.[31]

The social connection model seeks to articulate the intuition that we bear moral (and ultimately political) responsibility for our involvement in any social process that generates such domination and deprivation.

It makes sense, I think, to see the social connection model as an extension of the social contract model – Young stresses as a virtue of the social contract model the idea that social relationships are ontologically and morally prior to the formal constitution of political community.[32] Although Young's purpose is to leverage this idea of the ontological/moral priority of social over political relationship for purposes of generating an account of responsibility for global justice, I think that there is an important place for the social connection model of political responsibility even within already constituted political communities. As she argued influentially in her earlier work, especially *Justice and the Politics of Difference*, the problem of structural injustice is one with which liberal social contract theories of justice have difficulty coping because of their overreliance on formal procedural and distributive models of social justice and their failure to take into account structures of social power that are not easily captured in distributive terms and which are easily obscured in liberal theory's overly abstracted (and falsely neutral) characterization of individual parties to the social contract. (Indeed, given the forcefulness of her critique in earlier work, it is almost surprising to see her praise Rawls in particular and social contract theory in general in her late works.)

What a social connection model of political responsibility adds to the social contract model (again, without invalidating that model as a source of insight into the elements of social justice and political legitimacy) is its emphasis on the diffuse and complex nature of social structures whose outcomes are not necessarily intended or foreseen by the individuals who participate in them. The social connection model holds us morally responsible for the unjust outcomes generated by social structures regardless of whether we can specify how our actions contribute to the production of those injustices.

Colonial domination, exercised over a long period of time through a complex array of institutions and supported by often unconscious norms and assumptions, and maintained intergenerationally, clearly qualifies as a form of structural injustice within Young's framework, in addition to being constituted by overt and easily identifiable wrongs. The harms of colonial domination are many, but among its greatest harms is the one that Young identifies in the foregoing definition of structural injustice: the deprivation of the means to develop and exercise one's capacities. This consequence of colonialism – the profound damage to one's sense of agency even to the point of questioning whether one has capacities worth developing – is a common thread linking the experience of colonized people in all times and places.[33]

I won't explore here whether the structural injustices that exist within a political community generate a stronger moral duty to respond than do structural injustices through which we are connected to people with whom we do not share a political community, though it is a question that is well worth exploring. In general, however, a key contribution of the social connection model is its emphasis on a moral responsibility for *solidarity* with those whose capacities (or agency, individual and collective) have been impeded or damaged by structures of injustice.[34] An inquiry into the meaning of solidarity would take me beyond the scope of the present chapter; for present purposes, suffice it to say that I agree with J.L. Schiff (this volume) that Young's focus on the development and exercise of capacities as a central focus of responsibilities for structural injustice is a promising avenue for further exploration, and that it makes sense to turn from this emphasis to capabilities theory as developed by Amartya Sen and Martha Nussbaum.

Within a project of Canadian decolonization, the social connection model thus leads us to a view of political responsibility as solidarity with those who have been deprived of the means to develop and exercise their capacities. This further suggests a more specifiable responsibility to support Indigenous communities in their efforts to exercise and develop the capacities that they regard as most relevant for recovering and enhancing their agency both as individuals and as communities. In particular, it implies a responsibility to support the innovative work of Indigenous communities in developing structures of governance to replace Indian Act institutions with ones that generate political authority and capacity in a manner that harmonizes with traditional standards of legitimacy while also securing fiscal and political accountability to their members. Also, and relatedly, it implies supporting Indigenous communities' efforts to recover their languages and traditional knowledge.

The risk in this understanding of solidarity is the possibility that it will too easily collapse back into a colonial relationship in which European understandings of development and capability become the metric for the exercise of Indigenous capacities. Paternalism is not solidarity. For this reason, it seems vital that non-Indigenous support of Indigenous capacity building be led by Indigenous people's own definition of the capabilities they seek to exercise and develop, and their identification of the developmental resources (especially in the arena of training and education) that non-Indigenous people possess and might beneficially share.

I doubt that anyone feels the burden of responsibility for decolonization more keenly than Indigenous people themselves; it may be that in many instances the most valuable form of solidarity for non-Indigenous people to exercise is to get out of the way while also advocating for zones of autonomy or "zones of refuge"[35] within which Indigenous people can work out their own visions and practices of agency and self-empowerment.

As Schiff's chapter suggests, the social connection model's emphasis on capacities should also lead us to consider what capacities need to be developed in non-Indigenous people in order for us to be effective partners in solidarity, capable of responsiveness to the decolonizing efforts of Indigenous people themselves. Educating ourselves about the history and contemporary circumstances of settler colonialism is one dimension of the development of a decolonized settler consciousness – which further implies a particularly strong responsibility for decolonization among educators, who historically were among colonialism's principal agents. The duty to educate ourselves includes but goes beyond the responsibility (noted earlier as a corollary of the social contract model of political responsibility) to develop a widespread consciousness in settler society about our role as partners in treaty relationships with Indigenous peoples. The transformation of our own historical consciousness is thus, as Young argued, an indispensable element of the postcolonial project. Drawing on the work of Homi Bhabha, she writes,

> Hybridising the story of [the] relationship [between Indigenous people and settler populations] ... involves affirming colonial North America as a terrain of interaction, constructing [North] American subjectivity as ambiguous, and fashioning a relational understanding of historical jurisdictions.[36]

This call for hybridity leads me to conclude with a brief reflection on the relationship between the process of decolonization and the project of Enlightenment modernity. Avoiding the reproduction of a colonial relationship based on a presupposition that the capacities of settlers are superior to or more developed than those of Indigenous peoples requires a stance of humility towards our own knowledge claims. At the same time, it does not require that we abandon the bodies of knowledge developed through modern European forms of thought. We are all moderns now, Indigenous and non-Indigenous alike, and the challenge is to discover new forms of modernity both in our systems of knowledge and in our social-political orders that can coexist with rather than simply seeking to erase non-European structures of knowledge and order. As Dipesh Chakrabarty puts it, the point is not to eradicate Europe, but to provincialize it,[37] to honour its emancipatory aspirations but to recognize that the ideologies that generated and supported those aspirations also produced colonialism. Modernity has produced significant advances in human well-being, but it has also produced, *inter alia*, fascism, genocide, and potentially devastating climate change. Approaching Indigenous forms of knowledge, including Indigenous forms of political order, as sources of human wisdom from which we stand to learn – and *have* learned, though we remain largely unconscious of the fact – is a dimension of the process of decolonization from which we all may benefit immensely.

NOTES

1 The author wishes to thank participants in the Workshop on Political Responsibility held in conjunction with the Canadian Political Science Association Annual Meeting, Ottawa, May 27–29, 2009; colleagues in the Group on Indigenous Governance, University of Toronto; participants in the conference on How to Break Out of Colonialism, Project on Indigenous Peoples and Governance, Montreal, April 17–20, 2012; Joseph Carens, Victoria Freeman, Erica Frederiksen, Burke Hendrix, Genevieve Fuji Johnson, Loralea Michaelis, Peter Russell, Douglas Sanderson, and J.L. Schiff; and anonymous reviewers for responses to this chapter. I am conscious of the fact that I have not responded adequately to the many insightful comments I received from these colleagues and in these forums, and of course I bear full responsibility for the results. I also acknowledge with gratitude the financial support from the Major Collaborative Research Initiative on Indigenous Peoples and Governance, funded by the Social Sciences and Humanities Research Council of Canada.

2 Parliament of Canada, House of Commons, *Debates*, Thirty-ninth Parliament, 2nd Session, Vol. 142, No. 110 (Ottawa: Hansard), 6850.

3 A formal apology had been a political objective of Indigenous leaders and activists for many years. In the 1980s, residential school survivors began suing churches and the federal government for damages for the physical and sexual abuse they suffered in the schools and for the pain of being separated from their families and communities. This led the federal government to begin negotiating with Indigenous leaders and members of class actions, which culminated in the 2006 Indian Residential Schools Settlement Agreement between the federal government, the churches, the plaintiffs, and First Nations and Inuit representatives. The text of the

agreement is available at http://www.residentialschoolsettlement.ca/
Settlement.pdf. Its key provisions included monetary compensation to
survivors (the "Common Experience Fund"), funding for the Aboriginal
Healing Foundation (which supports projects for counselling for survivors
and their communities), and the establishment of the Truth and Reconciliation Commission. In the meantime, then–Indian affairs minister Jane
Stewart (in the Liberal government of Jean Chrétien) issued an expression
of "regret" for the residential schools policy in 1998, which was generally
regarded as a positive step but inadequate to the scale of the harm.

4 Two-thirds of Canadians believe that "individual Canadians with no
experience in Indian residential schools have a role to play in reconciliation between Aboriginal and non-Aboriginal people." Environics Research
Group, *2008 National Benchmark Survey*, prepared for Indian Residential
Schools Resolution Canada and the Truth and Reconciliation Commission,
May 2008, http://www.trc-cvr.ca/pdfs/benchmark_survey_f.doc. Interestingly, this view was held roughly equally by newcomers to Canada,
off-reserve Indigenous people, and the general population; support for the
statement was slightly weaker among on-reserve Indigenous people.

5 See, e.g., Pamela Palmater, "Stretched Beyond Human Limits: Death by
Poverty in First Nations," *Canadian Review of Social Policy* 65/66 (2011):
112–27.

6 According to Statistics Canada, approximately 60 percent of First Nations
people lived off-reserve at the time of the 2006 census. Many of these individuals live in urban areas. "Aboriginal Peoples in Canada in 2006: Inuit,
Métis and First Nations, 2006 Census," *The Daily*, Jan. 15, 2008, http://
www.statcan.gc.ca/daily-quotidien/080115/dq080115a-eng.htm.

7 See, e.g., Shannon Brennan, "Violent Victimization of Aboriginal Women
in the Canadian Provinces, 2009," in *Juristat* (Ottawa: Minister of Industry, 2011), http://www5.statcan.gc.ca.myaccess.library.utoronto.ca/
access_acces/alternative_alternatif.action?l=eng&teng=Violent%20victim-
ization%20of%20Aboriginal%20women%20in%20the%20Canadian%20
provinces,%202009&tfra=La%20victimisation%20avec%20violence%20
des%20femmes%20autochtones%20dans%20les%20provinces%20cana-
diennes,%202009&loc=/pub/85-002-x/2011001/article/11439-eng.pdf.

8 For an instructive overview of the historical processes and contemporary
structures of colonialism in Canada, see Gerald Taiaiake Alfred, "Colonialism and State Dependency," *Journal of Aboriginal Health* (November 2009):
45–54.

9 As Peter Russell pithily states the point, "[M]ake no mistake about it, Canada's Aboriginal peoples like their counterparts in other settler countries

are colonized peoples who had rule by a foreign power imposed upon them." "Indigenous Self-determination: Is Canada as Good as It Gets?," in *Unfinished Constitutional Business? Rethinking Indigenous Self-determination*, ed. Barbara Hocking (Canberra: Aboriginal Studies Press, 2005), 171.

10 The nonaccountability of the federal government to First Nations bands for their management of revenues from natural resources was recently upheld by the Supreme Court of Canada in Ermineskin Indian Band and Nation v. Canada, 2009 SCC 9 (February 2009).

11 Frances Abele, "Like an Ill-fitting Boot: Government, Governance and Management Systems in the Contemporary Indian Act," National Centre for First Nations Governance, July 2007, http://fngovernance.org/resources_docs/Analysis_of_Governance_and_Management_Under_the_Indian_Act.pdf, 30.

12 The National Centre for First Nations Governance, an Indigenous-led organization, is working with numerous communities to support their development of new institutions of self-government to replace Indian Act institutions. See http://www.fngovernance.org/. Federal funding for this centre was eliminated in the federal government's 2012 budget, along with funding for several other major institutions, such as the First Nations Statistical Institute and the National Aboriginal Health Organization, whose work supported evidence-based policy making in Aboriginal communities.

13 I should acknowledge that I am not here providing an analysis of the question of who possesses rightful title to land and resources, which is of course at the heart of disputes over land claims, and of scholarly debates over whether Aboriginal title ever existed or has been superseded by colonial conquest or other historical circumstances. I believe these issues to be well canvassed, and to my judgment well settled, in the existing theoretical and historical literature. For the theoretical debates around these questions, see Jeremy Waldron, "Superseding Historic Injustice," *Ethics* 103, no. 1 (1992): 4–28; Waldron, "Indigenity? First Peoples and Last Occupancy," *New Zealand Journal of Public and International Law* (2003): 55–82; Burke Hendrix, "Memory in Native American Land Claims," *Political Theory* 33, no. 6 (2005): 763–85; Hendrix, "Moral Error, Power, and Insult," *Political Theory* 35, no. 5 (2007): 550–73; and Douglas Sanderson, "Against Supersession," *Canadian Journal of Law and Jurisprudence* 24, no. 1 (2011): 155–82. For a legal and historical analysis, see Peter Russell, *Recognizing Aboriginal Title: The Mabo Case and Indigenous Resistance to English-settler Colonialism* (Toronto: University of Toronto Press, 2005). On the relationship between land and political self-determination, see Duncan Ivison, "Land, Law and

Governance," in *Postcolonial Liberalism* (Cambridge: Cambridge University Press, 2002), chapter 7.

14 Here, it is worth noting that Aboriginal people did not have the right to vote until 1960 and then they did not have the right to refuse incorporation as citizens into the Canadian state. Voter turnout among Aboriginal people is significantly lower than among the general population, and the efforts of the major national parties to woo them have waxed and waned from election to election.

15 For a thoughtful analysis, see Patrick Macklem, *Indigenous Difference and the Constitution of Canada* (Toronto: University of Toronto Press, 2001), 52–7. See also Mary C. Hurley, "The Crown's Fiduciary Relationship with Aboriginal Peoples," Parliament of Canada, Dec. 18, 2002, http://www.parl.gc.ca/content/LOP/ResearchPublications/prb0009-e.htm.

16 "Royal Proclamation of 1763," in *Revised Statutes of Canada* 2, no. 1 (Ottawa: Queen's Printer for Canada, 1985).

17 "The sui generis nature of Indian title, and the historic powers and responsibility assumed by the Crown constituted the source of such a fiduciary obligation ... [T]he Government has the responsibility to act in a fiduciary capacity with respect to aboriginal peoples. The relationship between the Government and aboriginals is trust-like, rather than adversarial, and contemporary recognition and affirmation of aboriginal rights must be defined in light of this historic relationship." R. v. Sparrow, 1 SCR 1075 (1990).

18 As Young advocates in, among other places, "Hybrid Democracy: Iroquois Federalism and the Postcolonial Project," in *Political Theory and the Rights of Indigenous Peoples*, ed. Duncan Ivison, Paul Patton, and Will Sanders (Cambridge: Cambridge University Press, 2000), 237–58.

19 See Glen Coulthard, "Subjects of Empire: Indigenous Peoples and the 'Politics of Recognition' in Canada," *Contemporary Political Theory* 6 (2007): 437–60.

20 Iris Marion Young, "Responsibility and Global Justice," *Social Philosophy and Policy* 23, no. 1 (2006): 116; see also Young, *Responsibility for Justice* (Oxford: Oxford University Press, 2011), 97.

21 For a persuasive membership theory of political apologies, see Melissa Nobles, *The Politics of Official Apologies* (New York: Cambridge University Press, 2008).

22 Young, "Responsibility and Global Justice," 118.

23 Ibid. Indeed, Steven Lukes would argue that domination is most complete and effective where the beneficiaries of unjust power relationships are not even understood as such. *Power: A Radical View*, 2nd ed. (Basingstoke: Palgrave Macmillan, 2005).

24 John Rawls, *A Theory of Justice* (Cambridge, MA: Harvard University Press, 1971), 102. The full passage reads: "The social system is not an unchangeable order beyond human control but a pattern of human action. In justice as fairness men agree to share one another's fate. In designing institutions they undertake to avail themselves of the accidents of nature and social circumstance only when doing so is for the common benefit."

25 What I'm getting at here is also akin to what David Miller discusses as community-based remedial responsibility in *National Responsibility and Global Justice* (Oxford: Oxford University Press, 2007), 104.

26 For a further discussion of treaty-based relationship between Canada's Indigenous peoples and settler society, see Russell, "Indigenous Self-determination."

27 For a discussion and interpretation of the Two-row Wampum, see Melissa S. Williams, "Sharing the River: Aboriginal Representation in Canadian Political Institutions," in *Representation and Democratic Theory*, ed. David Laycock (Vancouver: University of British Columbia Press, 2004), 93–118.

28 For an argument that the contract view and the fiduciary view are reconcilable, see Claire E. Hunter, "New Justification for an Old Approach: In Defence of Characterizing First Nations Treaties as Contracts," *University of Toronto Faculty of Law Review* 62 (2004): 61.

29 Or capacities. See Miller, *National Responsibility*, 103–4.

30 Delgamuukw v. British Columbia, 3 SCR 1010 (1997).

31 Young, *Responsibility for Justice*, 52 (emphasis added).

32 See, e.g., ibid., 139.

33 Quite possibly this damage to the sense of human agency constitutes the core of the injustice of all forms of domination.

34 As brought out in the title of one of Young's early articulations of the social connection view, "From Guilt to Solidarity," *Dissent* 50, no. 3 (Spring 2003). See also Young, *Responsibility for Justice*, 120–2.

35 Taiaiake Alfred and Jeff Corntassel, "Being Indigenous: Resurgences against Contemporary Colonialism," *Government and Opposition* 40, no. 4 (2005): 597–614.

36 Young, "Hybrid Democracy," 239. John Ralston Saul's recent book, *A Fair Country* (Toronto: Viking Canada, 2008), is a wonderful example of this sort of hybridization of Canadian consciousness. There, he argues that Canadians are at root a "Métis people" whose popular culture and moral sensibilities are deeply shaped by early encounters between settlers and Indigenous people but who went astray in the Victorian era by accepting the narrow-minded leadership of colonial elites.

37 Dipesh Chakrabarty, *Provincializing Europe* (Princeton, NJ: Princeton University Press, 2007).

6 Social Connections and Our Political Responsibilities to Future Generations

GENEVIEVE FUJI JOHNSON

Since the 1970s, a number of interesting writings have emerged concerning the moral status of future persons and generations and our responsibilities to them.[1] These writings raise several very difficult questions. For instance, how should we conceptualize our moral relationship to or with future persons and generations? Should we include consideration of them in decisions that could affect their lives? Should we consider them in public policy decisions that may have consequences for how they collectively live? If so, should we consider their rights or interests? Should we consider these rights or interests on par with ours? Are members of future generations our equals? Needless to say, while a fascinating area in moral and political philosophy, it is fraught with very challenging questions. Despite the profound conceptual and practical challenges, it is difficult to walk away from the idea that we have political responsibilities to future generations.

Indeed, the question "Do we have political responsibilities to future generations?" presents at least two perplexing challenges: (1) justifying the moral standing of future persons and generations, which is a necessary basis for our responsibilities to them (and, not to put too fine a point on this, but "them" is a reference to people who may or may not exist); and (2) reasonably identifying the content of these responsibilities when there is uncertainty about the long-term impact of many of our public decisions. This uncertainty is inherent because of the complexity of many policy areas and inevitability of continued social, cultural, political, economic, and environmental change.

In this chapter, I revisit this basic question and the challenges it poses.[2] I briefly survey utilitarian and deontological approaches to conceptualizing responsibilities to future persons and generations – approaches that ultimately I find not to rise to these challenges. Essentially, these approaches are too problematic in how they conceptualize the moral standing of future persons and too indeterminate in how they articulate responsibilities to them. I then explore Iris Marion Young's "social connection" model of political responsibility. Her model, which towards the end of her life she was developing with respect to contemporary generations, can yield important insights into the nature, scope, and kinds of responsibilities we have to future generations.

An approach to intergenerational responsibility premised on shared connections would be an improvement on existing approaches because it can provide a more concrete conception of the moral standing of future generations and more specific content for our responsibilities to them. The social connection model would ground moral standing and identify responsibilities in the relationships we establish with future generations in terms of what we anticipate to be shared experiences of benefits with them and what we forecast as burdens we will pass on to them. Relationships between present and future generations are not reciprocal in the same way as relationships among contemporaries. But relationships between generations can be characterized in terms of a certain kind of sharing. We have inherited from past generations many benefits – benefits that we should pass on to future generations as a matter of fairness. Moreover, we often rely on future generations to complete our projects. There is often an implicit reliance on future generations to continue, develop, or correct our public policies or, as the case may be, clean up the consequences of our public policies. Young's social connection model provides clarity concerning the significance of our intergenerational inheritance and dependency for the moral standing of future generations and for our responsibilities to them. Drawing from this model, we would be politically responsible to avoid or minimize the harmful consequences, and in particular structural injustices, associated with our publicly binding decisions for both existing and future generations to the extent that we share social connections. Young's model would thus provide a more focused and justifiable foundation for our responsibilities to future generations than existing models of intergenerational responsibility.

Utilitarian and Deontological Approaches

Gregory Kavka was among the first contemporary philosophers to treat the moral problems of futurity, which he understood largely in terms of the status and standing of future persons.[3] He argued that neither the temporal location of future persons nor our lack of knowledge about their interests justifies not treating them as our equals in the decisions we make. Future generations are our moral equals and should be treated as our moral equals. They should have standing in our decisions, and this standing should be on par with ours. According to Kavka, the equal moral standing and status of present and future persons imply that we have a full range of responsibilities to future generations. Specifically, this meant for Kavka that we should collectively aim to leave to our posterity a planet as rich in nature as that which we have inherited from our ancestors. Although an intuitively sound conclusion, it is woefully underdeveloped.

Since Kavka, theorists interested in exploring our moral relationships with and to future generations have tended to draw from two traditions of ethics: utilitarian and deontological. Utilitarianism's most basic claim is, in William Shaw's words, that "well-being or happiness is what really matters and, accordingly, the promotion of well-being is what morality is, or ought to be, all about."[4] Contemporary utilitarianism holds that the consequences of our actions should serve as the basis for evaluating them, and these consequences should be assessed in terms of the welfare they create.[5] Moral decisions should be made according to the impact they have on well-being, happiness, or utility. A utilitarian approach to decision making takes equally into account the welfare interests of each affected by a decision, combines these interests for each decision option, and concludes that the right option maximizes these interests. As John Rawls wrote, in teleological theories such as utilitarianism, "the good is defined independently from the right, and the right is defined as that which maximizes the good."[6]

For Peter Singer, the grounds for utilitarian moral standing are sentience and, more specifically, the ability to feel pain.[7] Utilitarian moral standing refers not only to human beings but also the whole range of sentient entities. From this perspective, species is no better a reason than sex, sexuality, race, ethnicity, or culture for excluding an entity's interests from moral consideration. Neither is current non-existence. To Singer, members of future generations who will come into existence, be sentient, and feel pain thus have moral standing. Singer seeks to make the "universe" better by reducing pointless suffering in "one particular place, at one particular time, than there would otherwise have been."[8] For Singer, "As long as we do not thereby increase suffering at some other place or time, or cause any other comparable loss of value, we will have had a positive effect on the universe."[9]

This basic idea animates the content for responsibilities to sentient creatures, existing and future. Welfare utilitarians seek specifically to maximize fundamental interests and resources, which they distinguish from more subjective desires and preferences. For Singer, the most important interests are "in avoiding pain, in developing one's abilities, in satisfying basic needs for food and shelter, in enjoying warm personal relationships, in being free to pursue one's projects without interference."[10] For Robert Goodin, "welfare interests refer to resources that prove useful to people whatever their ultimate ends."[11] Goodin views utilitarianism as premised ultimately on respect for an individual's preferences, interests, and dignity.[12] On this basis, Goodin provides substantive content to the utilitarian maxim by way of principles to inform the public distribution of welfare resources.[13] These include principles related to legal, socio-economic, and political guarantees to inform policy decision making such that the outcomes would not be to the unjustifiable detriment of a minority of people.[14] Goodin also includes ethical principles for decision making in areas of environmental policy, which would apply directly to future generations. These are avoiding irreversible outcomes, protecting vulnerable populations, maximizing the minimum pay-off, maximizing sustainable resources and benefits, and minimizing harm.[15]

As an approach to public decision making with far-reaching and long-term consequences, utilitarianism provides little justification for the moral standing of future persons. This very weak justification is exemplified in debates between those in favour of maximizing the total and those in favour of maximizing the average welfare. In the context of a fixed and stable number of affected persons, this question poses no problem. However, in the context of intergenerational responsibilities, the implications of this decision can be very contentious. The contentious issues relate directly to the question of "Who counts?" Who has moral standing? Persons who will exist or persons who could exist?

One possible way to increase total happiness is to increase the number of people in the world to its carrying capacity. As Shaw writes, this total view implies that "1) that we have some positive obligation to have children, 2) that, other things being equal, the more people on earth, the better, and 3) that in principle increasing the number of people can offset a decrease in people's happiness."[16] This view implies that we grant moral standing to future people who could exist. Given its counter-intuitive implications, we may instead have responsibilities to try to ensure that everyone who exists or who will exist is as happy as possible. On this view, utilitarian responsibilities are to actual persons existing either in the present or in the future, and they would include not bringing persons into a world where they will surely lead suboptimal but still marginally happy lives. Unlike a total happiness view, this average interpretation would not justify an increase in numbers of happy persons without considering how happy they are likely to be given social and environmental conditions. However, maximizing average happiness has its own problems. For example, as Shaw writes, "average-happiness utilitarianism implies, implausibly, that in a world of very happy people, it would be wrong to bring into existence a moderately happy person because doing so would lower average happiness."[17] Also problematically, the average happiness view implies that we have a duty to procreate if our prospective offspring will be happier than average. The standard of maximizing average happiness, moreover, implies that it would be good if people whose happiness is below average were eliminated.

Beyond the problems of granting moral standing to future persons and generations in either total or average terms, another problem with a utilitarian approach is the broad and indeterminate nature of welfare interests. The claim that all persons have generalized interests in clean water and air, adequate nutrition, sufficient biodiversity and biological resources, and healthy ecosystems is convincing. However, identifying and articulating welfare interests in specific policy contexts, which are inhabited by policy actors from different cultural backgrounds and with different ideological views, may reveal very different opinions on what these are and on how to maximize them. Utilitarianism provides little direction as to how to address this indeterminacy of welfare interests in light of genetic, social, cultural, and moral change. Humans will evolve genetically and socially, and this evolution will have implications for their needs and interests. The fact of uncertainty, which increases the further into the future we cast our moral thinking, means that we can never really know what will constitute, or how to realize, the welfare of those who could be affected by our public policies. "Welfare interests" is too broad a category to be helpful in specific areas of public decisions.

Philosophers often contrast utilitarianism (or, more broadly, teleology) with deontology. Rawls defines a deontological theory as "one that either does not specify the good independently from the right, or does not interpret the right as maximizing the good."[18] Generally, in deontological theories, the right is prior to the good. In other words, the right imposes certain restrictions on conceptions of the good held by individuals so that all can pursue their good on fair and equal terms. When deontologists refer to these restrictions, they speak about axioms that are right in and of themselves. Rawls captures the essence of modern deontology, writing that each "member of society is thought to have an inviolability founded on justice or, as some say, on natural right, which even the welfare of everyone else cannot override."[19] From an axiom of moral equality, contemporary deontologists argue that persons have certain rights that correspond to duties or responsibilities of other persons, societies, or governments.

Jeremy Waldron argues that rights are requirements generated by the fundamental interests of persons. These fundamental interests relate to the ultimate value in realizing "choice, self-determination, agency, and independence," as well as to the acquisition of certain socioeconomic goods.[20] Conceptualizing rights as claims or requirements deriving from the fundamental interests of persons, Waldron highlights the special role they play in defining responsibilities and obligations. As Waldron writes, we should reserve the language of rights for interests that have "*special* importance, an importance which would warrant overriding other values and ideals whenever they conflict with the protection of rights."[21] Essentially, claim rights are requirements to uphold fundamental interests deriving from the moral dignity or autonomy of persons.

What is the basis of deontological moral standing and is it more convincing than that of utilitarianism? Most deontologists take not merely sentience but more specifically conation or rationality to be the determinant of moral standing. Joel Feinberg, for example, defines conative life as consisting of conscious wishes, desires, and hopes, as well as unconscious drives, latent tendencies, and natural fulfilments.[22] The specific dimensions of conative life give rise to corresponding rights that should be upheld. For Feinberg, all humans and some non-human animals can have moral standing expressed in terms of rights. Rawls speaks even more specifically of the moral standing of persons, who for him can be only human beings. According to Rawls, moral personality consists of powers to develop a sense of justice and conception of the good.[23] In virtue of persons having these powers to "the requisite minimum degree to be fully cooperating members of society," they are equal.[24] Equal justice requires that their interests be fairly considered in a system of social cooperation. While deontologists vary in their perspectives on the relative importance of sentience, conation, and rationality, they converge on the claim that persons have moral standing and that this moral standing is a potentiality that will be realized in due course. This potentiality can suffice in granting deontological moral standing to both existing and future persons.

Brian Barry develops three theorems based on the fundamental moral equality of persons, which consist of a set of responsibilities and obligations to members of future generations. The first maintains that each person, regardless of when and where she exists, has a moral claim to equal rights. As Barry notes, existing generations are able to affect the "likelihood that there will be equal rights in the future."[25] The more environmental degradation and pollution we leave our successors, for example, the poorer their prospects for a range of rights equal to ours. The second theorem relates to the responsibility of individual choice. For Barry, individual choice, insofar as it takes place within the context of a just system of legal rights, resources, and opportunities, justifies inequalities of outcome. Barry thus writes that people in the future cannot be held responsible for the physical conditions that they inherit, "so it would seem ... unjust if people in the future are worse off in this respect than we are."[26] As a corollary to this second theorem, Barry develops the principle of compensation, which holds that unjust inequalities must be mitigated by ensuring equal opportunities for future generations. Where this is not possible, members of future generations should be compensated for the loss of these opportunities. Barry's third theorem articulates a list of vital interests to provide substance to the claims to equal opportunities of both existing and future generations. This list includes "adequate nutrition, clean drinking-water, clothing and housing, health care and education" and so on,[27] and derives from an understanding of what it means to be human (at least according to Barry). If humans exist, they will surely have vital interests in "certain objective requirements for human beings to be able to live healthy lives, raise families, work at full capacity, and take a part in social and political life."[28]

Similar to utilitarian approaches, deontological approaches to responsibilities and obligations to future generations are problematic in terms of moral standing. The challenges to granting future persons moral standing in terms of rights, liberties, and opportunities rest on the premise that only actual beings, and not possible beings, can have such claims. Critics argue that only actual persons have sentience, conation, and rationality; thus, only actual persons can have fundamental interests. For example, Ruth Macklin's position is that interests are not *a priori* but are specific to persons existing within a particular context.[29]

She argues that it is the interests of actual persons – that is, interests in fulfilling person-specific capacities in a particular socio-historical setting – that constitute the basis for ascribing rights. Without reference to actual existence, it is epistemologically impossible to determine the form and substance of interests and therefore of rights. From a somewhat different angle, Hillel Steiner argues that future people cannot have rights because they cannot exercise them.[30] Steiner argues that the formal features of rights are "implied in our speaking of rights, like abilities, as being exercised."[31] His argument is that rights give us certain powers to demand that others fulfil correlative duties and to waive the compliance of others with these duties. A future person is both physically and logically unable to exercise his or her rights, and unable to demand or waive fulfilment of the duties of a present person. Therefore, Steiner holds, he or she cannot be understood to have rights. Like Macklin and Steiner, Richard de George holds that only once a being exists does it have rights.[32] Moreover, he insists that a being cannot have a reasonable claim to what is neither possible nor available at the time of its conception.[33] His claim is twofold: not only does it not make sense to ascribe rights to members of future generations before they come into existence, but also it does not make sense to ascribe rights to capabilities that will be either impossible or unavailable to future generations when they come into existence.[34]

Beyond problems with their conceptions of moral standing, there are problems with deontological perspectives on the content of responsibilities and obligations to future generations. Like utilitarian theories of the good, deontological perspectives on fundamental interests inevitably tend to be too indeterminate. There is too much uncertainty stemming from the inevitable genetic, social, cultural, and moral change that will take place over the course of a lengthy time frame. The fact of this uncertainty means that we can never know in precise terms what will constitute, let alone how to protect, the vital interests of those who could be affected by our public policies. Although deontology supplies a universal theory of the good that is convincing at a generalized level, this good is too broad to be meaningful in specific contexts of public decisions.

Contributions from the Social Connection Model

Similar to the utilitarian and deontological theorists whom I've covered, Iris Marion Young did not assume that obligations of justice hold only between "those living under a common constitution within a single political community."[35] I argue in the following paragraphs that Young's model could extend political responsibility beyond the confines of constitutions and communities located not only across space but also across time. It could provide us with a conception of responsibilities to future generations that overcomes some of the problems confronted by utilitarianism and deontology. Young's model recognizes that some harms are caused by and come to people because of their participation in social processes that transcend boundaries. Young focused on obligations of global justice arising from the structural inequalities caused in and because of these processes among contemporaries. She conceptualized her model of responsibility with direct reference to the transnational processes of production, distribution, and marketing of clothing that were based ultimately on the exploitation of piecemeal laborers. Given important similarities between global and intergenerational forms of justice – similarities such as the interconnections between local decisions and far-reaching consequences, and the corresponding distance between those who have responsibilities and those to whom they are responsible – Young's model can provide resources with which to address some of the challenges associated with conceptualizing how morally we ought to treat future generations and how we might fulfil these responsibilities. By focusing on social and economic connections, it can offer a more applied conception of the moral standing of and our political responsibilities to future generations than utilitarian and deontological approaches. In particular, we can locate the basis for our responsibilities to future generations in Young's emphasis on the inevitability of shared connections and the importance of awareness, reciprocity, and deliberation within them to avoid or minimize structural injustices.

Young drew from theories of social structures and structural processes to develop her model. In her most basic articulation, a social structure implies an interconnected set of institutional rules and routines, a mobilization of resources, and shared infrastructures.[36] Differentiated social positions are established by and across this structure. Young was especially interested in the structure of continuous processes of production, investment, and trade connecting people across the world that create and sustain unequal power hierarchies and an unjust distribution of material resources.[37] Young was aware that these connections confer benefits as well as burdens on individuals, which can both expand and contract the possibilities for individuals' existence and their pursuit of conceptions of the good. The connections among members of these structures provide both the enablements of and constraints on individuals' possibilities for fulfilment. For Young, injustices occur in terms of the way in which structures constrain and enable these possibilities. As she wrote, the "constraints and enablements occur not only by means of institutional rules and norms enforced by sanctions, but by means of incentive structures that make some courses of action particularly attractive and carry little cost for some people, or make other courses of action particularly costly for others."[38] Structural injustice transpires when these processes systematically serve in dominating or in threatening to dominate large collectivities of people. Specifically, it transpires when domination or threats of domination created or perpetuated by these processes deprive some people of opportunities to develop and fulfil their capacities while enabling other people to maximize their opportunities.[39]

It is a stretch to conceptualize our relations with future generations in terms of reciprocity and deliberation within social processes and structures. Obviously, we don't share with future generations a temporal context as we participate in these processes and structures. But, in a way, we do share with them. Indeed, we do pass on to future generations social norms and conventions, institutional rules and routines, resources, and infrastructures. We inherit these as well. For example, Canadians have inherited a constitution similar in principle to that of the United Kingdom. Canadians continue to uphold a number of constitutional and political norms inherited from the British. To take additional examples from the field of medicine, children born in the past several decades have inherited vaccines against polio, measles, mumps, and rubella. We've also inherited the means for less invasive surgeries, including laparoscopic techniques. And we've inherited astonishing diagnostic imagining capabilities. Superconductivity, applied in MRIs, was discovered a century ago. Beyond medical advances, all of us have inherited a wealth of cultural ideas and materials in the form of music, poetry, literature, painting, sculpture, and architecture from ancient societies. We have no justifiable entitlement to squander this collective inheritance and effectively to prohibit future generations from enjoying its benefits. We should share it equitably with future generations.

Of course, we've also inherited burdens. The environmental and economic are the most obvious. We may be on the verge of the next major mass extinction of species. Debts and deficits throughout the world continue to balloon. You could also say that Americans have inherited a complex web of profoundly racialized social norms from a history of slavery. Canadians too have inherited dimensions of colonialism seen in the extremely disproportionate rates of poverty and incarceration among Aboriginal peoples. Clearly, we have certain relationships – political relationships insofar as they are among collectivities, centre on the distributions of societal benefits and burdens, and impact on the shaping of our identities and social positioning – with past generations. Collectively, we should be aware of and deliberate on the benefits and burdens we've inherited from them and those we pass on to future generations.

Indeed, we have a certain political relationship with future generations. Existing generations are reliant on future generations. Many of our public decisions and policies are based on either a stated or unstated understanding that future generations will solve the problems we create. Future generations enable us, in a way, to make and act on decisions. For example, it is arguable that nuclear energy would not have been developed in the 1960s and implemented in the 1970s had policy makers, governments, and citizens not been prepared to defer economic costs, technological challenges, and political battles to future generations. Early proponents of nuclear energy depended on future generations for the short-, medium-, and, most costly and complex, long-term management of nuclear waste. They depended on future generations in order to develop and implement this technology – a technology that has provided previous, provides current, and will provide future generations with enormous benefits (especially as we shift away from carbon-based forms of electricity generation) but that also raises enormous ethical questions, costly technological challenges, and very contentious political issues.

There is no doubt that Young included a temporal dimension into her model of responsibility. She did so both implicitly and explicitly. Temporality figures implicitly in her model as a rebuking of a nondeliberated acceptance and passing on of norms. For Young, structural inequalities exist and continue to exist in part because of a collective complicity in inheriting, accepting, and passing on certain "background" conditions that contribute to the occurrence of injustice. As she wrote, we "contribute to a greater or lesser degree to the production and reproduction of structural injustice precisely because we follow the accepted and expected rules and conventions of the communities and institutions in which we act."[40] We do so from habit, without explicit reflection and deliberation on what we're doing, why we're doing it, and the broader consequences of doing it. Instead, we focus on our immediate goals, how to achieve them, and with whom we need to interact to achieve them. Young was sensitive to our inheritance of certain norms that may be oppressive and to our lack of attention to how we may be passing them on with respect to the people with whom we interact. She thus heightened our awareness that, in many of our decisions concerning the consumption of goods and services, we fail as individuals to reflect seriously and as collectivities to deliberate publicly on implications for people distant in space, and to this we can add time.

The temporal dimension is more explicit in Young's sensitivity to historical contexts as defining social processes that enable us to fulfil opportunities but that also constrain us and cause structural injustices. Current global economic, environmental, and cultural conditions, she wrote, "are the products of previous actions, usually products of many coordinated and uncoordinated but mutually influencing actions."[41] The effects of these collective actions can be either beneficial or detrimental for existing and future generations. With respect to the global garment industry, she noted that the impoverished conditions of the lives of young piecemeal laborers are the "structural consequences of decisions and aggregated economic processes beginning more than three decades ago."[42] For Young, it

is not merely the case that the actions and interactions of differently positioned persons, drawing on the rules and resources the structures offer, take place on the basis of past actions whose collective effects mark the physical conditions of action; these actions and interactions also often have future effects beyond the immediate purposes and intentions of the actors.[43]

Political responsibility for Young is thus grounded in the past but oriented towards the future.

Young's moral standing is based directly on collective participation in processes that could result in structural inequalities. Young focused on processes in the global garment industry that exploit piecemeal labour in sweatshops littered around the world. Participation in these processes delimits who is responsible, to whom, for what, and how. Those who participate in exploiting cheap labour markets to maximize their profit margins and those who buy products made by laborers working in terrible conditions for barely subsistence pay are responsible for addressing the structural inequalities created through these processes. As consumers, our responsibilities include educating ourselves about the conditions in which items are produced, boycotting certain corporations, lobbying governments for distributive justice, and working in our own individual ways to alleviate global poverty. Essentially, we have responsibilities to the individuals we directly and indirectly exploit in the processes specific to the global garment industry. Participation in other processes, in which existing generations benefit while future generations are burdened, could serve similarly to delimit moral standing and political responsibilities.

For example, to return to the case of nuclear energy, millions of North Americans benefit from this form of electricity generation. Currently, however, there is no long-term waste management or disposal site to contain the highly radioactive waste from the hundreds of generators across the continent. We are, effectively, passing these economic, technological, political, legal, and environmental burdens on to future people. Drawing from Young's model, we could argue that those who may be affected by these burdens should have moral standing in our decisions concerning the continued generation of electricity from this source and concerning the plans we develop for the safe disposal of used nuclear fuel. This could, of course, include many people, present and future, given the nature of hazards associated with high-level radioactive waste, which can be very long-lived. Nonetheless, this conception of moral standing applies not to all those who could exist but to all those who could be directly, negatively affected. This would include members of communities that currently host nuclear energy facilities and of communities in, around, and en route to prospective waste disposal sites. We know enough about the geological conditions necessary for a long-term site. And we know that various communities have inhabited and will continue to inhabit the few geographical areas in North America suitable for a long-term site. Moral standing would in this case, and in others, be confined to specific policy decisions and delimited by the adequate forecasting of their consequences.

Drawing from Young's model, we would not have to worry about our broad responsibilities to future generations writ large; we should, however, worry about our responsibilities to future generations in light of the harms we may cause them because of our participation in policy-specific processes. Young's model recognizes, in a way that neither the utilitarian nor the deontological model does, a subset of people to whom we have specific obligations and responsibilities. A theory of intergenerational responsibility based on Young's understanding of shared connections would include a conception of moral standing relatively narrow in scope, thus avoiding difficult questions that utilitarian and deontological approaches confront.

Similarly, this shared connection approach would improve on utilitarian and deontological conceptions of responsibilities. Intergenerational responsibilities derived from shared connections would be more focused, based specifically on the social connections we establish with and structural inequalities we could create for future generations. The basic principle of Young's model is that all agents who contribute to the structural processes that produce injustice have responsibilities to try to avoid, minimize, or remedy these injustices. On her model, we would not have blanket obligations to minimize the suffering of everyone, everywhere. We would not have undifferentiated obligations to everyone and special obligations to no one. Young brought into focus connections in which we can cause harm and injustice to people differentially situated in space (i.e., across the globe). She wrote that

> while everyone in the system of structural and institutional relations stands in circumstances of justice that give them obligations with respect to all the others, those institutionally and materially situated to be able to do more to affect the conditions of vulnerability have greater obligations.[44]

We can extend this understanding of connections to include people situated across time (i.e., in future generations). Again, the case of nuclear energy and nuclear waste management provides a concrete example of specific responsibilities we could derive from an application of Young's model of social connection. Given the nature of hazards associated with the nuclear generation of electricity and the waste it creates, our responsibilities would be to ensure that we carefully and transparently monitor the nuclear energy industry and that we develop and implement a system for the disposal of nuclear waste that is safe over the very long term. This would entail ensuring adequate investment in research, modelling, and testing to develop and implement the technology that best achieves this objective to the extent that we are capable of foreseeing. Given the costs associated with maintaining this technology, we would also have to ensure that we put away adequate funds for future generations. In addition, this model would entail more specific responsibilities to future generations who inhabit geographic locations that are *en route* and close to disposal sites we decide to develop. These responsibilities could include compensation for appropriated lands.

Moreover, Young's model would offer a more circumscribed understanding of responsibilities than Goodin's or Barry's. Instead of speaking broadly to the importance of avoiding irreversible decisions, protecting vulnerable populations, and ensuring access to clean water, as the latter do, Young's model would direct us to consider our collective decisions in terms of the benefits we derive from them and the structural injustices they cause in specific practices, processes, and institutions. As implied by Young, we should of course exercise diligence and precaution in our collective decision making, which would entail attempts to forecast the fundamental interests and basic rights of future people and to make scientifically sound and socially acceptable assessments concerning the potential impacts of our decisions on future people. On Young's model, we would do so with direct reference to the decisions that we partake in and the detrimental consequences that we are reasonably able to predict. As Young noted, it may be very difficult at best and impossible at worst to trace "the particular causal relationship of the actions of particular individuals or organizations to structural outcomes."[45] This uncertainty only increases the farther into the future we cast the scope of our understanding of political responsibility. In some cases, we may be simply unable to forecast the long-term consequences.

When we cannot forecast, to the best of our collective abilities, a reasonably sound range of outcomes of a given policy decision, this may be because the connection between ourselves and our future generations is too diffuse. It may be because we cannot envision shared experiences relating to the benefits and burdens of a given decision. In such cases, our responsibilities extend only to partaking in inclusive and informed public deliberations on the need for such decisions. We must, of course, be responsible for the justificatory onus for our decisions with uncertain and unknown consequences. If we collectively determine that we need to make such a decision, despite due diligence in both public deliberations and expert risk analysis, and despite the limitations of our knowledge and intractability of uncertainty, we are not responsible. In these cases (for example, increasing the production of genetically modified crops if that were the only way to address a global food shortage), because we cannot know the consequences of a given decision, we cannot respond and are therefore not responsible. Another way of putting this is that we are responsible only for the inclusive and informed collective deliberation on the need for such a public decision, for exercising due diligence when attempting to determine and assess a broad range of consequences associated with it, and for publicly and reasonably justifying it. We are not responsible for consequences that fall beyond our collective ability to forecast and assess the risks associated with a decision we justifiably need to make. Where we can foresee harmful consequences associated with our decisions, however, our responsibilities would be to take measures to avoid or minimize these. On Young's model, we would thus limit our potentially unlimited responsibilities to future generations.

Another insight into the nature and content of our responsibilities to future generations is Young's understanding of the political. She noted that structural injustices result not from single decisions or acts but from decisions, actions, and policies of collectivities. This is helpful in clarifying the political nature of responsibilities of global justice *and* of intergenerational justice. As she wrote,

> Structural injustice occurs as a consequence of many individuals and institutions acting in pursuit of their particular goals and interests, within given institutional rules and accepted norms. All the persons who participate by their actions in the ongoing schemes of cooperation that constitute these structures are responsible for them, in the sense that they are part of the process that causes them.[46]

Hundreds of millions of us contribute to structural inequalities that take place across space and time. As such, our responsibilities are to those we affect and those we could affect, and our responsibilities are shared. Young highlighted for us that each of us is partially responsible for the harmful outcomes, and for the risks of harmful outcomes, of decisions made by the collectivities of which we are a part. But she also noted that our roles in exploitative processes and structures differ and that, consequently, our individual responsibilities differ. Some of us rightfully bear a greater burden of responsibility than others, depending on our particular role in these processes and structures. In any case, our responsibilities are discharged only through collective action. They entail changing the processes and institutions involved in giving rise to hazards, harms, and injustices. Since these changes can occur only through collective endeavours, we have a responsibility to work together to make them.

Once again, with reference to nuclear energy, our responsibilities would be to engage in a broad public debate on it, including the nature, magnitude, and probabilities of hazards associated with it. Historically, governments opting for nuclear energy have treated this form of electricity generation as a case of a high magnitude but very low probability risk. On this basis, they have justified deriving enormous benefits from it. However, the March 2011 earthquake and tsunami off the coast of northeastern Japan and the partial meltdown and explosions at the Fukushima Daiichi power plant reveal that, in some cases, the magnitude of potential harms ought to be a significant basis on which to decide against a given technology. We know nuclear energy is dangerous, and we know that nuclear waste is very difficult to contain and can remain fatally toxic for thousands – even hundreds of thousands – of years. We know that our collective decision to derive electricity from this energy source places existing and future generations in perilous circumstances. We are connected to existing persons across the globe and future persons across time by the processes and institutions that enable us to produce and derive benefit from nuclear energy. Our collective responsibilities in this case are thus to consider phasing it out and making larger investments in the research and development of less hazardous and more sustainable forms of energy. Insofar as we decide we need this source of energy, we must minimize the risks to both existing and future generations. Young's model enables us to clarify this sentiment and rationalize it as a moral basis for publicly binding policy.

Conclusion

It is insightful to read Young's work on global justice and political responsibility with reference to our relations with, or relation to, future generations. A theory of intergenerational responsibility based on Young's understanding of shared connections would help us address some of the very difficult questions concerning future generations. In particular, Young's conception of moral standing and political responsibility is more circumscribed, and as such more helpful, than that of utilitarianism or deontology. Our decisions, actions, and policies (and lack thereof), taking place in terms of specific social processes and institutions, can impact in serious and detrimental ways on distant persons. This impact can be understood in terms of structural injustice. This basic contribution is helpful because it encourages us as members of collectivities to deliberate on not merely our immediate aims but also the longer-term consequences of our decisions. Within our schemes of social cooperation, each of us expects and should expect others to consider the impacts of decisions on the conditions of justice for all of us. These schemes are extensive, but they are also circumscribed by specific processes and institutions. Young's writings, as always, remain moving because they speak to the moral equality of all persons and to realizing that equality in the face (or faces) of oppression. Young was deeply concerned with the well-being of existing persons and generations. We can also imagine her being equally concerned with the well-being of future persons and generations. The overarching goal of her work, and its most significant contribution, was to aid in alleviating the suffering of marginalized people. In her final works, she sought to delineate a basis for our shared political responsibility to realize this goal.

NOTES

1 See, for example, Bruce Edward Auerbach, *Unto the Thousandth Generation: Conceptualizing Intergenerational Justice* (New York: Peter Lang, 1995); Andrew Dobson, ed., *Fairness and Futurity: Essays on Environmental Sustainability and Social Justice* (Oxford: Oxford University Press, 1999); Avner de-Shalit, *Why Posterity Matters: Environmental Policies and Future Generations* (London: Routledge, 1995); Ernest Partridge, ed., *Responsibilities to Future Generations: Environmental Ethics* (Buffalo: Prometheus Books, 1981); and Richard Sikora and Brian Barry, eds., *Obligations to Future Generations* (Philadelphia: Temple University Press, 1978). See also Genevieve Fuji Johnson, "Discursive Democracy in the Transgenerational Context and a Precautionary Turn in Public Reasoning," *Contemporary Political Theory* 6 (2007): 67–85, and Johnson, *Deliberative Democracy for the Future: The Case of Nuclear Waste Management in Canada* (Toronto: University of Toronto Press, 2008).
2 See Genevieve Fuji Johnson, "Discursive," and Johnson, *Deliberative Democracy*, for an earlier discussion of these issues.
3 Gregory Kavka, "The Futurity Problem," in Sikora and Barry, *Obligations to Future Generations*, 180–203.
4 William Shaw, *Contemporary Ethics: Taking Account of Utilitarianism* (London: Blackwell, 1999), 10.
5 Amartya Sen and Bernard Williams, introduction to *Utilitarianism and Beyond* (Cambridge: Cambridge University Press, 1982), 4.
6 John Rawls, *A Theory of Justice* (Cambridge, MA: Belknap, 1971), 24.

7 Peter Singer, "The Concept of Moral Standing," in *Ethics in Hard Times*, ed. Arthur Caplan and Daniel Callahan (New York: Plenum, 1981), 33.

8 Peter Singer, *How Are We to Live?: Ethics in an Age of Self-interest* (Oxford: Oxford University Press, 1997), 231.

9 Ibid.

10 Peter Singer, *Practical Ethics* (Cambridge: Cambridge University Press, 1979), 27.

11 Robert Goodin, *Utilitarianism as Public Philosophy* (Cambridge: Cambridge University Press, 1995), 13n36.

12 Robert Goodin, *Political Theory and Public Policy* (Chicago: University of Chicago Press, 1982), 73.

13 See ibid. and Goodin, "Ethical Principles for Environmental Protection," in *The Moral Dimensions of Public Policy Choice: Beyond the Market Paradigm*, ed. John Martin Gillroy and Maurice Wade (Pittsburgh, PA: University of Pittsburgh Press, 1992), 411–25.

14 Goodin, *Political Theory and Public Policy*, chapter 5, passim.

15 Goodin, "Ethical Principles for Environmental Protection," 411.

16 Shaw, *Contemporary Ethics*, 33.

17 Ibid., 32.

18 Rawls, *Theory of Justice*, 30.

19 Ibid., 28.

20 Jeremy Waldron, ed., *Theories of Rights* (Oxford: Oxford University Press, 1984), 8.

21 Ibid., 14.

22 Joel Feinberg, "The Rights of Animals and Unborn Generations," in Partidge, *Responsibilities to Future Generations*, 143.

23 John Rawls, *Political Liberalism* (New York: Columbia University Press, 1993).

24 Ibid., 19.

25 Brian Barry, "Sustainability and Intergenerational Justice," in *Fairness and Futurity: Essays on Environmental Sustainability and Social Justice*, ed. Andrew Dobson (Oxford: Oxford University Press, 1999), 98.

26 Ibid.

27 Ibid., 97.

28 Ibid.

29 Ruth Macklin, "Can Future Generations Correctly Be Said to Have Rights?," in Partridge, *Responsibilities to Future Generations*, 151–5.

30 Hillel Steiner, "The Rights of Future Generations," in *Energy and the Future*, ed. Douglas MacLean and Peter G. Brown (Totawa, NJ: Rowman and Littlefield, 1983), 152.

31 Ibid.

32 Richard De George, "The Environment, Rights, and Future Generations," in Partridge, *Responsibilities to Future Generations*, 157–65.
33 Ibid., 160.
34 Ibid., 159.
35 Iris Marion Young, "Responsibility and Global Labor Justice," *Journal of Political Philosophy* 12 (2004): 365–88, and Young, "Responsibility and Global Justice: A Social Connection Model," *Social Philosophy and Policy* 23 (2006): 102.
36 Young, "Responsibility and Global Justice," 111.
37 Ibid., 105.
38 Ibid., 114.
39 Ibid.
40 Ibid., 120.
41 Ibid., 113.
42 Ibid.
43 Ibid., 114.
44 Ibid., 106.
45 Ibid., 122.
46 Ibid., 114.

7   Political Practices as Performances of Political Responsibility

TANJA PRITZLAFF

Introduction

In her 2004 article "Responsibility and Global Labor Justice," Iris Marion Young spells out the criteria for a conception of political responsibility that she distinguishes from a liability model of responsibility.[1] One of the major differences between these two conceptions lies in the fact that, according to Young, the liability model of responsibility does not apply to the production of structural injustice. The liability model "derives from legal reasoning to find guilt or fault for a harm"[2] and is based on the idea of individually attributable actions. This line of thinking assigns "responsibility to particular agents whose actions can be shown as causally connected to the circumstances for which responsibility is sought."[3] Young's model of political responsibility, on the other hand, shifts the focus to complex, co-produced social structures whose outcomes cannot be causally connected to intentional individual actions. It "does not seek to mark out and isolate those to be held responsible, thereby distinguishing them from others, who by implication then are not responsible."[4] While the liability model is based on the idea of individual, intentional actions that can be assigned to specific agents who are responsible for them, the model of political responsibility applies to structural processes that cannot be related to individualized instances of guilt or fault for a harm. In fact, structures that produce injustice are often maintained through contributory acts of thousands or even millions of people who, at the individual level, "may be going about their business in a normal way and not intending to do any harm."[5] The production of structural injustice may therefore be regarded as a "cumulative effect"[6] of individual actions that, by themselves, may seem "normal and acceptable."[7] By "acting according to normal rules and accepted practices," individuals contribute to the production of unjust circumstances.[8] According to Young, it is "the nature of such structural processes that their potentially harmful effects cannot be traced directly to any particular contributors to the process."[9]

Therefore, a practice that maintains and renews structures of injustice cannot be characterized as an intentional action at the individual level. By contrast, it is a complex, co-produced "collective activity of individual social actors whose final product ... is qualitatively different from the sum of its parts."[10] By performing contributory acts to these kinds of practices on an everyday basis, actors contribute to structural injustice – oftentimes without even knowing it. On the other hand, though, co-produced, collective day-to-day activities may also be regarded as a remedy for structural injustice: oppositional political practices that embody political responsibility may change complex structural processes that are in need of improvement by actually fulfilling the actions required to bring about change.

In this chapter, I aim at a deeper understanding of a conception of political practices as co-produced performances of political responsibility. Although Young uses the notion of "practices" several times, it is not one of her core concepts. And while she refers to collective activities that are needed in order to change structural processes that produce unjust outcomes, she doesn't provide a systematic definition of these collective activities, nor of the collective activities that add up to structural processes that produce unjust outcomes. In my view, the concept of practice expresses the need to focus on complex forms of collective action when it comes to political responsibility. A systematic definition of the concept of practice, therefore, strengthens Young's conception of political responsibility, since on the one hand it identifies a level of collective activities that produce the structural processes which are in need of change, and on the other hand it defines the level of political interactions that have to be performed in order to bring about change.

Through a distinction between an explicit and an implicit dimension of the normativity of practices, I hope to provide an understanding of the normative forces at work at the microlevel of political interaction, ranging from habitual rule following and compliance to conscious protest. Relations of responsibility are maintained and updated through microlevel interactions between people occupying different institutional or social positions in society. The conception of political practices as co-produced actualizations of implicit norms presented in this chapter rests on an understanding of practice that stems from a social theoretical approach referred to as "practice theory."[11] Young develops her version of political responsibility as shared responsibility in the context of cases of structural injustice. Therefore, it seems promising to take a closer look at the ways in which actual practices embody, preserve, or renew these structures by following "normal rules" – or the ways in which they may serve as a means to put these structures at risk, to overcome unjust structures. In this context, the relation between practices and normativity is of crucial importance.

The practice-based approach presented in this chapter reflects the constant challenge to substantiate normative principles, like the principle of responsibility, in actual political practice. Yet it also gets at the "relevance of revealing norms that are in place"[12] – that is, it points out how particular practices shape the embodied realities of people living under unjust conditions by uncovering the norms and values inherent in those practices. To do that, a distinction between two dimensions of normativity – explicit normativity in the sense of rule following and implicit normativity that is maintained and updated within processes of social interaction – seems to be helpful. This two-dimensional conception of normativity strengthens Young's account of responsibility as a shared, collective-action-based concept, since it spells out the relation between norms and actual co-produced practices. Young doesn't treat this relation in a systematic way, but rather implicitly or by way of example.

As a first step, I outline the key features of Young's conception of political responsibility. I then introduce the distinction between two dimensions of the normativity of practices, the explicit and the implicit dimension. The third and final step attempts to integrate Young's model of political responsibility and the two-dimensional version of normativity into a conception of political practices as performances of political responsibility.

Young's Conception of Political Responsibility

In the context of her analysis of global labour justice,[13] Young focuses on the so-called "anti-sweatshop movement." In the framework of this movement, activists have assigned responsibility for unjust working conditions in the global apparel industry not only to the local employ-ers and brand name companies who operate apparel manufacturing facilities with poor working conditions, but also to the retailers and consumers in highly industrialized states who sell and buy the prod-ucts produced under these poor working conditions in other parts of the world. At a first glance, it is obvious that retailers and consumers in the western world cannot be made liable in a legal sense for selling or buying these products, since they do not perform actions that violate the law, or even act in the way they do in order to intentionally harm other people – for example, in the Philippines or Bangladesh. They sim-ply go "about their business in a normal way and not intending to do any harm"[14] by selling and buying clothes. These practices on a day-to-day basis, however, although not based on individual intentions to do harm or on actions that might be regarded as a crime in the legal sense, contribute to structural injustice. But can, for example, people who buy or sell T-shirts from certain brands be considered responsible for the poor working conditions in factories in other parts of the world where these T-shirts are produced? In the context of questions like these, Young introduces a conception of responsibility that is distinct from a liability model of responsibility. The aim of this conception is, as Young puts it, to make sense of "any claims of responsibility that mem-bers of a society might be said to have toward harms and injustices of distant strangers."[15] Young convincingly outlines that within a "domi-nant conception of responsibility as liability,"[16] these claims make little sense. Therefore, she elaborates a conception of responsibility that she refers to as political responsibility.

Young makes a clear distinction between the model she calls the li-ability model of responsibility and her own conception of political re-sponsibility. The liability model of responsibility "derives from legal reasoning to find guilt or fault for a harm."[17] Under this model, as Young explains, one

> assigns responsibility to particular agents whose actions can be shown as causally connected to the circumstances for which responsibility is sought. This agent can be a collective entity, such as a corporation, but when it is that entity can be treated as a single agent for purposes of assigning responsibility.... The liability model is primarily backward-looking in its purpose; it reviews the history of events in order to assign responsibility, often for the sake of exacting punishment or compensation.[18]

The last point of this characterization of the liability model of responsibility is especially relevant for a conception of political practices as performances of political responsibility. The liability model, as Young conceives it, relies on a consideration, interpretation, and evaluation of past events. The actions undertaken to promote responsibility are reactions to specific actions by specifiable agents that can be shown to be causally connected to harmful outcomes.[19] These reactions consist in assigning responsibility for past actions to specific agents. Furthermore, they usually have the function of "absolving other agents who might have been candidates for fault."[20]

In addition, the fact that the liability model of responsibility is grounded in legal reasoning brings about a strong connection to explicit rules and norms. As I will outline later, an understanding of the normativity of actions that restricts itself to conduct in the sense of rule following is too narrow. Practices in the sense of complex, collective activities of a large number of people incorporate an implicit dimension of normativity that constrains and enables agents in their actual performances of their contributory acts to those practices.

Young's conception of political responsibility is more comprehensive in the sense that it extends the scope of responsibility to the actual day-to-day practices of agents, to the normative accountability of everyday actions and routines – like selling or buying T-shirts from certain brands – that cannot be referred to as wrongdoings in a legal sense. According to the model of political responsibility, "finding one responsible does not imply finding one at fault or liable for a past wrong, but rather refers to agents' carrying out activities in a morally appropriate way and aiming for certain outcomes."[21] By integrating the implicit moral appropriateness of lawful everyday actions into her conception of responsibility, Young introduces a forward-looking element to the concept of responsibility that implies the requirement to act not only according to explicit rules like laws, but also according to implicit norms of appropriateness that also apply to normal everyday practices that are lawful in a legal sense, but contribute to outcomes that are wrong in a moral sense.

However, although the liability model as presented by Young derives from legal reason, her critique of it is not restricted to a way of thinking about responsibility in terms of simply imposing legal sanctions on individuals who caused harm by performing actions that are unlawful in a legal sense. The target of her critique, in a broader sense, is the whole idea that it is always possible to identify specific, individualizable perpetrators. In the case of structural injustice, this approach is insufficient not only because of its law-based character but also because it is based on oversimplification. To blame specific agents for structural processes that produce injustice, accordingly, seems to be nothing more than an easy way out.[22]

It is important to point out that Young's model of political responsibility does not aim at replacing the liability model.[23] On the contrary, Young underscores the importance of this first layer of responsibility:

> A concept of responsibility as blame or liability is indispensable for a legal system and sense of moral right that respects agents as individuals and expects them to behave in respectful ways toward others. When applying this concept of responsibility, there must be clear rules of evidence, not only for demonstrating the causal connection between this agent and a harm, but also for evaluating the intentions, motives, and consequences of the actions. By proposing a social connection model of responsibility, I do not aim to replace or reject the liability model of responsibility.[24]

Some criticisms expressed regarding Young's model thus seem to be based on a misunderstanding.[25] Young introduces her social connection model of responsibility because "where there is structural social injustice, a liability model is not sufficient for assigning responsibility."[26] Young identifies five main features of this model. The model (1) is not isolating; (2) includes judgment of background conditions; (3) is more forward- than backward-looking; (4) contains an understanding of shared responsibility; and (5) holds that these responsibilities are discharged only through collective action.[27]

With regard to the first feature, according to Young the liability model of responsibility is based on the assumption that it is possible and necessary to isolate those who are responsible for specific harms and to distinguish them from others who are not responsible. But, as Young points out, in cases in which "harms result from the participation of thousands or millions of people in institutions and practices that produce unjust results ... such an isolating concept of responsibility is inadequate."[28] In cases of structural injustice, responsibility may vary in degree, but it is not possible to absolve others entirely from blame or responsibility.

In terms of the second feature, as Young outlines, the liability model of responsibility implicitly assumes a "normal background situation that is morally acceptable, if not ideal."[29] Crimes or wrongdoings for which specific agents are held responsible are interpreted as deviations from normality. The reactions to those crimes or wrongdoings – that is, forms of punishment – are, therefore, attempts to restore normality. A model of political responsibility, on the other hand, that focuses on the connections that agents have to structural injustices "does not evaluate harm that deviates from the normal and acceptable, but rather often brings into question precisely the background conditions that ascriptions of blame or fault assume as normal."[30] The model of political responsibility, thus, reflects on our "normal" day-to-day practices and routines – like buying or selling T-shirts – that contribute to structural injustices.[31]

With regard to the third feature, in the context of the liability model, sanctions and punishments are applied in reaction to a specific past action that is unlawful in a legal sense. Therefore, the liability model can be described as "primarily backward-looking."[32] The model of political responsibility, on the other hand, is characterized by Young as forward-looking in the sense that it answers to structural injustices by enjoining "those who participate by their actions in the process of collective action to change it."[33] However, Young herself provided some hints in her writings that a sharp distinction in this backward-looking/forward-looking sense is not possible.[34] Accordingly, this inexactness within her characterization of the two models – that is, with regard to the "retrospective/prospective portion of the distinction" – has been met with criticism.[35]

The fourth feature is essentially that "all those who contribute by their actions to the structural processes producing injustice share responsibility for these harms."[36] Shared responsibility is defined by Young not in the sense of collective responsibility, but in the sense of "a personal responsibility for outcomes or the risks of harmful outcomes, produced by a group of persons. Each is personally responsible for outcomes in a partial way, since he or she alone does not produce the outcomes; the specific part that each plays in producing the outcome cannot be isolated and identified, however, and thus the responsibility is essentially shared."[37]

Finally, with regard to the fifth feature, this shared nature of responsibility leads to the fact that "forward looking responsibility can be discharged only by joining with others in collective action."[38] Structural processes that produce unjust outcomes can be altered only if "many actors in diverse social positions work together to intervene in them to produce different outcomes."[39] Indeed, "many of those properly thought to be victims of harm or injustice may nevertheless share ... political responsibility in relation to it,"[40] since their actions contribute to the structural processes that produce injustice. They share responsibility for "helping to bring about change."[41] The idea of political responsibility, therefore, rests on the assumption that agents occupying different institutional and social positions coordinate their actions and engage in co-produced, oppositional political practices in order to achieve change. Young writes:

> What might be required from one's position is doing something different from or additional to the tasks normally assigned to that position, but different persons nevertheless stand in differing positions in structures that produce unjust outcomes, which afford them different opportunities and capacities for influencing those outcomes.[42]

Practices are performed by various agents whose contributory acts to these practices vary with respect to their differing positions. However, although to a different degree, they can all make a difference when it comes to the outcome of practices in the sense of complex, collective activities.

If one takes a closer look at the five main features of Young's model, it becomes apparent that it is founded on a concept of agency that questions the appropriateness of our "lawful" day-to-day practices and routines. In the context of her example, the global apparel industry, she assigns responsibility even to those who tend to be regarded as passive victims of economic globalization. The suggested shift from treating certain groups of people as passive victims of globalization to treating them as active participants, as "agents empowered to have control over their lives,"[43] also implies a broader conception of doing politics and acting politically. The concept of political practices, in this sense, cannot be restricted to certain types of official or governmental actions.[44] If day-to-day routines of textile workers in developing countries and consumer behaviour in industrial countries are means to either reproduce or to change contexts of structural injustice, these microlevel practices are to be understood as political practices as well.

Although Young disagrees with Hannah Arendt on the question of whether the ground of political responsibility "lies in being members of the same nation-state,"[45] her conception of political responsibility is based on Arendt's concept of collective political responsibility.[46] Young outlines that, as does Arendt in many contexts, I mean by "political" something broader than government. In addition, by politics or the political I am referring to the activity in which people organize collectively to regulate or transform some aspect of their shared social conditions, along with the communicative activities in which they try to persuade one another to join such collective action or decide what direction they wish to take it. The sort of responsibility that anti-sweatshop activists claim that they, their fellow consumers, and specific institutions of manufacture or distribution of goods have is political responsibility in this sense.[47]

Understood in this broad sense of politics or the political, differently situated people occupying different institutional or social positions in society are committed and enabled to perform in a way that is appropriate to the norm of shared responsibility – through their actual, embodied day-to-day practices and routines. Within a framework of shared responsibility and collective action, relations of responsibility are maintained and updated through microlevel practices in social interactions.

It is, of course, obvious that not every agent involved in interactions that lead to structural injustice has the same opportunities and capacities to bring about change. In this sense, although those who share responsibility are all in some sense responsible, the responsibility varies in kind and degree. Different agents have "different kinds of responsibilities in relation to particular issues of justice, and some arguably have a greater degree of responsibility than others."[48] These differences correlate, as Young puts it,

> with an agent's position within the structural processes. By virtue of this structural positioning, different agents have different opportunities and capacities, can draw on different kinds and amounts of resources, or face different levels of constraint with respect to processes that can contribute to structural change.[49]

Young identifies four parameters along which agents can reason about their actions in relation to structural injustice: power, privilege, interest, and collective ability.[50]

For Young, politics in the context of political responsibility means, first and foremost, "public communicative engagement with others for the sake of organizing our relationships and coordinating our actions most justly."[51] As Young was able to show on a broader level in *Inclusion and Democracy*, the participation in political practices is dominated by power asymmetries resulting from structural positioning.[52] The degree to which, for example, the ability to engage in public communication constrains or enables specific agents depends not only on compliance with explicit laws or rules of conduct but also on acting according to implicit, context-dependent norms of appropriateness and correctness within our everyday practices. Therefore, the norms inherent in political practice have to be addressed at a broader level and cannot be reduced to mere compliance with laws or rules. If one interprets political practices as basic elements of an understanding of forward-looking, political responsibility, agents who engage in political practices are faced with a constant challenge to redefine and to justify their respective commitments and entitlements within the political process. Political practices, in this sense, are actualizations of implicit, context-dependent norms of appropriateness and correctness, and in the case discussed here they can be interpreted as actualizations of norms with regard to the appropriateness and correctness of contributory acts that add to cumulative outcomes of structural processes – like structural injustice in the global apparel industry.

Explicit and Implicit Normativity

In political theory, the grounds of justification for political actions – that is, the sources of normativity – are often characterized in terms of governance by explicit rules in a community's behaviour, values, or preferences. What Young describes as the liability model of responsibility can be understood in this sense: explicit rules – that is, laws – guide our actions, and in cases in which specific agents violate the law, reactions follow in terms of sanctions. Compliance with those explicit rules is interpreted as a state of normality, and deviations are exceptions that have to be addressed by performing specific reactions – that is, sanctions. In addition, compliance or non-compliance with those explicit rules is interpreted as intentional, conscious compliance or non-compliance. Agents consciously and intentionally follow explicit rules or violate explicit rules. The way to understand the normative status of a practice in the sense of correct or incorrect is constructed through a relation to a general, explicit, law-like rule. But, if the normativity of practices is perceived exclusively as manifesting itself in references to explicit rules, a crucial feature of the normative forces at work at the microlevel of interaction is neglected: the procedural, context-dependent actualization of implicit norms of appropriateness and correctness that guide our everyday practices. A distinction between an explicit and an implicit dimension of the normativity of practices may provide an understanding of the entirety of the normative forces at play.

Explicit Normativity

If we think of the grounds of justification for actions – that is, the sources of their normativity – laws and rules are the first things that come to our mind. Agents justify their actions and decisions by explicitly referring to laws and formal regulations. Existing laws and regulations – laws and regulations that are in force at the time actions are performed and decisions are made – exert a normative force that is somehow conferred upon newly established regulations or performed actions. A regulation gains its normative force through the act of referring to other, previously made regulations. But this seems to be only one – although the most obvious – case of what we might think of under the heading of explicit normativity.

The term explicit normativity as I understand it comprises a range of sources agents explicitly refer to in order to support a claim, to justify an action, to substantiate a claim if challenged, or to normatively underpin a proposed option to act. Explicit references brought forward in discourse serve as argumentative backing for a position; they support objections in favour of or against a certain option. By explicitly referring to a normative source, agents promote the establishment of a common basis of commitment. In addition, they point out that by performing their actions in a certain way, they consciously follow a certain rule or violate a certain rule. If an agent refers to an explicit norm, his or her actions can be individually traced back to a given reason.

Following Christine Korsgaard[53] a suggestion would be to identify a range of fundamental sources of normativity agents explicitly refer to. But although the outline of a range of explicit normative resources – that is, a perspective that exceeds a mere reference to legal norms or laws – opens up a broader perspective on the sources agents might refer to as grounds of justification for their actions, these resources constitute only one component of a more comprehensive structure.

Conceptions that characterize normativity solely in terms of laws, rules, or regularities seem to identify normativity with a "special kind of entity."[54] As Robert Brandom puts it, Kant's model of how to understand the normative status of correct and incorrect rests on the assumption that "what makes a performance correct or not is its relation

to some explicit rule."[55] In Brandom's words, according to this conception, correctness is assessed by making a reference to "a rule or principle
that determines what is correct by explicitly saying so."[56] According to
Brandom, this view "that proprieties of practice are always and everywhere to be conceived as expressions of the bindingness of underlying
principles ... may be called regulism about norms."[57] What Brandom
describes as regulism about norms might, in this context, be characterized as a one-dimensional conception of normativity, a conception
incorporating only explicit sources of normativity.

Following Brandom's criticism, Joseph Rouse, one of the most prominent advocates of "practice theory,"[58] suggests an "alternative, 'normative' conception of practices."[59]

IMPLICIT NORMATIVITY

On Rouse's conception, the constitutive elements of a practice are integrated within the practice by "complex relations of mutual interaction."[60] The contributory acts performed by the respective individual
agents who co-produce the practice constitute the practice as a whole,
but a practice is more than a sheer accumulation of individual acts. The
norms that guide the contributory acts of the respective participants
cannot be completely traced back to context-independent, general
norms that individual agents comply with. As already mentioned, a
practice has to be conceived as a complex, co-produced "collective activity of individual social actors whose final product ... is qualitatively
different from the sum of its parts."[61] A practice has a complex, holis-
tic character. Practices can be defined as typical patterns of interaction,
and these patterns "constitute something at issue and at stake in their
outcome."[62] What is at stake in those practices is, as Rouse puts it, "per-
spectivally variant or open-textured":[63]

> On such accounts, the normativity of practices is expressed not by a deter-
> minate norm to which they are accountable but instead in the mutual ac-
> countability of their constitutive performances to issues and stakes whose
> definitive resolution is always prospective ... Normativity on such a con-
> ception is an essentially temporal phenomenon. It amounts to a mutual
> interactive accountability toward a future that encompasses present cir-
> cumstances within its past.[64]

Implicit normativity, in this sense, doesn't rely on an understanding of normativity as consisting of "determinate norms" individual

agents comply with, but on an understanding that stresses the temporal, context-dependent, responsive character of normativity. While engaging in a practice, agents interact with one another in "complex patterns of mutual responsiveness."[65] The implicit, procedural dimension of normativity has, as Rouse describes it, to be maintained and updated in the actual processes of interaction. Performances respond to one another through acts of correction and repair, through the drawing of inferences, through acts of translation, feedback loops, reward or punishment of a performer, by trying to replicate an act in different circumstances, mimicking it, and so on.[66] Rouse's underlying understanding of normativity is a very broad one.[67] He conceives normativity in terms of "how we hold one another accountable to what is at issue and at stake in ongoing practices."[68]

If one adopts this idea of an implicit, procedural dimension of normativity, explicit sources of normativity have to be complemented by a conception of political practices as performative actualizations of implicit norms. This idea of a two-dimensional conception of normativity can be elaborated in analogy to Young's two-layered conception of responsibility, as consisting of rule-based liability and practice-based political responsibility. A two-dimensional conception of the normativity of practices has to address the relation between sources agents explicitly refer to when justifying their actions and the implicit normative force that becomes apparent in what they actually do, the norms they observe, perpetuate, and respond to in their actual engagement in political practices – for example, buying or not buying products of certain brands in the apparel industry. Explicit normative resources constitute, in this sense, only one dimension of the normativity of practices. Agents refer to explicit norms, but at the same time they maintain, preserve, and renew the normative forces at work at a second level of normativity.

These ideas suggest that a comprehensive understanding of political normativity has to encompass two dimensions of normativity: an explicit and an implicit dimension. In this conception, the reference to explicit norms is complemented by an implicit dimension that is expressed through "complex patterns of mutual responsiveness."[69] By picturing political normativity in this way, the reductive conception exhibited by a regulism about norms[70] can be underpinned by a normative base that is located in our actual, co-produced day-to-day practices. In this sense, even everyday routine practices – like shopping – can be regarded as contributory acts to political practices.

Political Practices as Performances of Political Responsibility

Following Young's model of political responsibility, a conception of political practices as performances of political responsibility can be outlined that comprises the aforementioned two dimensions of normativity as well as a more inclusive understanding of forms of political practices, ranging from habitual rule following and compliance to conscious protest. As Young points out, implicit norms – norms that can be characterized as exclusionary[71] – often guide our ideas about the range of moderate or decent ways of engagement in political discourse. In Young's view, political practices should encompass alternative forms and dimensions of activities. In accordance with this broader conception of political practice, Young refers to politics or the political as "the activity in which people organize collectively to regulate or transform some aspect of their shared social conditions, along with communicative activities in which they try to persuade one another to join such collective action or decide what direction they wish to take it."[72] According to Young, creative acts of protest or other alternative modes of expression – like the forms of protest used by the anti-sweatshop movement – can contribute to a more inclusive form of communicative engagement.[73] In the sense of changing society through society,[74] Young suggests adopting alternative norms and social practices in the political sphere. Politics, therefore, should take an open stance towards learning from successful forms of social practices.[75] Especially political practices that aim at transforming oppressive social and political structures – in the sense of oppositional, performative political practices[76] – often express themselves in these alternative ways.

At a very fundamental level, our everyday interactions are guided by implicit norms, and these implicit norms, therefore, also affect the way we act politically. If one includes alternative forms of communication and expression into a conception of political practices as performances of political responsibility, it is important to base this conception on an understanding of normativity that comprises norms not only in the sense of explicit rules but also in the sense of implicit norms that guide our day-to-day activities.

One of the main aims of including alternative forms of communication into a conception of political practice is, following Young, to enable "communication across differentiated structural positions."[77] A conception of political practices as performances of political responsibility, therefore, has to promote an understanding of political practices as acts that integrate and function against the background of structurally asymmetrical positions. The idea of political practices that bring about change has to incorporate the idea of functioning against the background of an asymmetric allocation of power and other resources – that is, knowledge and communicative skills. Furthermore, an elaborate conception of political practices as performances of political responsibility has to incorporate the idea of, to rephrase Drexler's formulation, political action that performs responsibility rather than asks for it.[78] Political responsibility, in this sense, is actualized and comes into being through the performance of significant political practices.

Conclusion

According to Young, being "responsible in relation to structural injustice means that one has an obligation to join with others who share that responsibility in order to transform the structural processes to make their outcomes less unjust."[79] While Young identifies this obligation as the core idea of political responsibility, her conception of the actual performances that bring about change remains rather vague. It is obvious, though, that she is talking neither about individual actions nor about a sheer aggregate of individual actions. What she has in mind is a form of collective action that corresponds to the "essentially shared nature of the responsibility."[80] In my view, the nature of complex, collective performances that lead to structural injustice as well as the nature of performances that transform structural processes and make their outcomes less unjust can best be captured by the concept of practices.

Practices in this sense cannot be sufficiently understood if they are conceived as actions that comply with or violate explicit rules or laws. Political practices are also actualizations of implicit norms that guide our co-produced day-to-day interactions and routines – complex, context-dependent patterns of mutual responsiveness that cannot be pictured as the result of individual, conscious, and intentional acts of rule following. Implicit normativity is woven into the fabric of political practices – as a dimension of normativity that is temporal and always actualized in practice through the mutual accountability of the contributory acts that constitute the practice. Following Young's distinction between a liability model of responsibility and a model of political responsibility, the liability model conceives the norm of responsibility in an explicit, law-like sense. In contrast, Young's model of political responsibility perceives responsibility in a sense that it performs responsibility rather than asks for it. According to this model, responsibility is actualized through significant political practices. In the case of structural injustice, shared responsibility is actualized through "joining with others in collective action,"[81] through collective, co-produced political practices that bring about improvement and change. Young's conception of supplementing a liability model of responsibility with a model of political responsibility is closely related to the idea that the norms that guide our day-to-day actions cannot be reduced to laws and explicit rules. It is also closely related to the dimension of collective – as opposed to individual – action. Within contexts of complex structural injustice, the norms implicit in our day-to-day practices in the sense of collectively produced activities are of vital importance, too. Therefore, the idea presented in this chapter is to integrate the aforementioned concept of practice and its two-dimensional version of normativity into a conception of political practices as performances of political responsibility.

NOTES

1 Iris Marion Young, "Responsibility and Global Labor Justice," *Journal of Political Philosophy* 12, no. 4 (2004): 365–88, http://dx.doi.org/10.1111/j.1467-9760.2004.00205.x. Young further elaborates this line of thought in chapter 9 of her book *Global Challenges: War, Self-determination, and Responsibility for Justice* (Cambridge: Polity, 2007) and in chapter 4 of *Responsibility for Justice* (Oxford: Oxford University Press, 2011). (See also Young, "From Guilt to Solidarity: Sweatshops and Political Responsibility," *Dissent* 50, no. 2 (2003): 39–44, and Young, "Responsibility and Global Justice: A Social Connection Model," *Social Philosophy & Policy* 23, no. 1 (2006): 102–30, http://dx.doi.org/10.1017/S0265052506060043.)

2 Young, "Responsibility and Global Labor Justice," 368.

3 Ibid.

4 Ibid., 377.

5 Martha C. Nussbaum, foreword to *Responsibility for Justice*, by Iris Marion Young (Oxford: Oxford University Press, 2011), xii.

6 Young, *Responsibility for Justice*, 151.

7 Martha C. Nussbaum, "Iris Young's Last Thoughts on Responsibility for Global Justice," in *Dancing with Iris: The Philosophy of Iris Marion Young*, ed. Ann Ferguson and Mechthild Nagel (Oxford: Oxford University Press, 2009), 136.

8 Ibid.

9 Young, *Responsibility for Justice*, 100.

10 Alessandro Duranti, "The Audience as Co-author: An Introduction," *Text* 6, no. 3 (1986): 239, http://dx.doi.org/10.1515/text.1.1986.6.3.239.

11 Theodore R.Schatzki, Karin Knorr Cetina, and Eike von Savigny, eds., *The Practice Turn in Contemporary Theory* (London: Routledge, 2001); Andreas Reckwitz, "Towards a Theory of Social Practices: A Development in Culturalist Theorizing," *European Journal of Social Theory* 5, no. 2 (2002): 243–63, http://dx.doi.org/10.1177/13684310222225432; David G. Stern, "The Practical Turn," in *The Blackwell Guide to the Philosophy of the Social Sciences*, · ed. Stephen P. Turner and Paul A. Roth (Malden, MA: Blackwell, 2003), 185–206; and Joseph Rouse, "Practice Theory," in *Philosophy of Anthropology and Sociology*, ed. Stephen P. Turner and Mark W. Risjord, Handbook of the Philosophy of Science (Amsterdam: Elsevier, 2007), 639–81.

12 Christine M. Koggel, "Agency and Empowerment: Embodied Realities in a Globalized World," in *Embodiment and Agency*, ed. Sue Campbell, Letitia Meynell, and Susan Sherwin (University Park: Pennsylvania State University Press, 2009), 258.

13 Young, "From Guilt to Solidarity"; idem, "Responsibility and Global Labor Justice"; idem, "Responsibility and Global Justice"; Young, *Global Challenges*; and Young, *Responsibility for Justice*.

14 Nussbaum, foreword, xii.

15 Young, "Responsibility and Global Labor Justice," 366.

16 Ibid.

17 Ibid., 368.

18 Ibid. According to Young, conceptions of "moral responsibility, both among scholars of ethics and in ordinary language, most often assume a liability model of responsibility. While people often distinguish between holding people morally responsible for a circumstance and regarding them as criminally or civilly liable in legal terms, their conception of responsibility is similar in form. To say that an agent is responsible means that they are blameworthy for an act or its outcome. The conditions for holding an agent morally responsible are similar to those of legal responsibility: we must be able to show that they are causally connected to the harm in question and that they acted voluntarily and with sufficient knowledge of the consequences." Young, *Responsibility for Justice*, 97–8.

19 "The liability model of responsibility causally connects the circumstances for which responsibility is sought with specific actions of particular agents. In this sense the liability model individualizes even when the agent it

identifies is a corporate entity." Young, "Responsibility and Global Labor Justice," 375.

20 Young, *Responsibility for Justice*, 97–8.

21 Young, *Global Challenges*, 175.·

22 As Young puts it, a public discourse of blame "oversimplifies, failing to develop a public understanding of the actions and practices whose consequences produce injustice. The power of some actors is improperly inflated, and that of many others is ignored" (Young, *Responsibility for Justice*, 117). The act of blaming, in this sense, is also studied as a psychoanalytic phenomenon: "To blame is not the same as the discovery of defects or inefficiencies within a causal network, or the discovery of faults or breaks in the system. To blame is magically to short-circuit the recognition of multiple determinants or actual defects in the system itself. To blame is a leap to 'discover' simple causes which are thought to be acts of intentional evil. In the sense that psychoanalysis sees events as psychologically determined, the search for single sources of evil is absurd. But in the sense that psychoanalysis retains concepts of freedom of choice, then, of course, one can imagine choices by individuals which at least most people would regard as evil. Perhaps this apparent antinomy can be resolved if traditional concepts of morality itself can be rethought. Perhaps blaming systems can be replaced by responsibility systems." Vann Spruiell, "On Blaming: An Entry to the Question of Values," *Psychoanalytic Study of the Child* 44 (1989): 245.

23 "Political responsibility adds to rather than replaces this first layer of responsibility." Young, "Responsibility and Global Labor Justice," 382. As Ann Ferguson points out, Young's concept of political responsibility supplements the liability model of responsibility. Ann Ferguson, "Iris Young, Global Responsibility, and Solidarity," in Ferguson and Nagel, *Dancing with Iris*, 187.

24 Young, *Global Challenges*, 174.

25 Regina Kreide, for example, defends the importance of the liability model against Young's conception of political responsibility and bases her critique of Young's conception on the assumption that Young *rejects* the liability model. Regina Kreide, "Gibt es eine gerechte Weise, ein T-Shirt zu produzieren? Verantwortung und globale Gerechtigkeit bei Iris Marion Young," in *Jahrbuch der Heinrich-Böll-Stiftung Hessen e.V.*, vol. 9, *Gesellschaftliche Perspektiven: Bildung, Gerechtigkeit, Inklusion*, ed. Peter Niesen and Margret Krannich (Essen: Klartext Verlag, 2009), 98. In contrast, Young herself points out that her argument "is not that the concept of political responsibility should replace that of a fault or liability model, but should

supplement that model in analyses of responsibility in relation to structural processes." Young, "Responsibility and Global Labor Justice," 368.

26 Young, *Global Challenges*, 175. "The liability model relies on a fairly direct interaction between wrongdoer and wronged party. Where structural social processes constrain and enable many actors in complex relations, however, those with the greatest power in the system, or those who derive benefits from its operations, may well be removed from any interaction with those who are most harmed in it. While it is usually inappropriate to *blame* those agents who are connected to but removed from the harm, it is also inappropriate, I suggest, to allow them (us) to say that they (we) have nothing to do with it. Thus, I suggest that we need a different conception of responsibility to refer to the obligations that agents who participate in structural social processes with unjust outcomes have. I call this a social connection model." Young, *Global Challenges*, 175.

27 Ibid., 176–80. See also Young, "Responsibility and Global Labor Justice," 388, and Young, *Responsibility for Justice*, 104–13.

28 Young, *Global Challenges*, 176.

29 Ibid.

30 Ibid., 177.

31 "When we judge that structural injustice exists, we mean that at least some of the normal and accepted background conditions of action are not morally acceptable. Most of us contribute to a greater or lesser degree to the production and reproduction of structural injustice precisely because we follow the accepted and expected rules and conventions of the communities and institutions in which we act. Usually, we enact these conventions and practices in a habitual way, without explicit reflection and deliberation on what we do, having in the foreground of our consciousness and intention immediate goals we want to achieve and the particular people we need to interact with to achieve them." Ibid., 177.

32 Young, "Responsibility and Global Labor Justice," 378.

33 Young, *Global Challenges*, 178.

34 "To be sure, such backward-looking condemnation and sanction may have a forward-looking purpose; we may wish to deter others from similar action in the future, or we may wish to identify weak points in an institutional system that allows or encourages such blameworthy actions, in order to reform the institutions. Once we take this latter step, however, we have left a liability model and are moving toward a conception of political responsibility." Ibid., 378.

35 Nussbaum, "Iris Young's Last Thoughts," 141–2. See also Nussbaum, foreword, xx–xxv. Rainer Forst comments on Young's claim that the social

connection model, unlike the liability model of responsibility, is forward-
rather that backward-looking, in the following way: "I would, however,
think that this is only a difference of degree; for one of her main insights
was, I take it, that injustice has a name, i.e., that it is identifiable, even if
only roughly. And to construct justice as she does, on the basis of a critical
analysis of existing structures of powerlessness and exploitation, does not
just mean ending injustice but also addressing it retrospectively. And even
though this can never be done in the detailed way that 'absolute justice'
would demand, a historical account is an essential part of the story of
(in)justice we tell, and it implies demands of redress and compensation.
If justice is situated in a social-historical and structural context, narratives
of injustice have to be the basis of the construction of just institutions,
it seems to me." Rainer Forst, "Radical Justice: On Iris Marion Young's
Critique of the 'Distributive Paradigm,'" *Constellations* 14, no. 2 (2007): 263,
http://dx.doi.org/10.1111/j.1467-8675.2007.00437.x.

36 Young, *Global Challenges*, 179.
37 Ibid.
38 Ibid.
39 Ibid.
40 Ibid., 180.
41 Young, "Responsibility and Global Labor Justice," 387.
42 Ibid., 385.
43 Koggel, "Agency and Empowerment," 267.
44 Young, *Responsibility for Justice*, 112.
45 Ibid., 377. In Young's view, the "scope of issues of justice corresponding
    to political responsibility derives not from the boundaries of a state or
    political jurisdiction, but from the connections generated by the structural
    processes." Young, "Responsibility and Global Labor Justice," 388.
46 Hannah Arendt, "Collective Responsibility," in *Responsibility and Judgment*,
    ed. Jerome Kohn (New York: Schocken Books, 2003), 147–58.
47 Young, "Responsibility and Global Labor Justice," 377.
48 Young, *Global Challenges*, 183.
49 Ibid.
50 Ibid.
51 Ibid., 179.
52 Iris Marion Young, *Inclusion and Democracy* (Oxford: Oxford University
    Press, 2000).
53 Christine M. Korsgaard, *The Sources of Normativity* (Cambridge: Cambridge
    University Press, 1996), http://dx.doi.org/10.1017/CBO9780511554476.
    "We live under the pressure of a vast assortment of laws, duties,

obligations, expectations, demands, and rules, all telling us what to do. Some of these demands are no doubt illicit or imaginary – just social pressure, as we say (as if we knew what that was). But there are many laws and demands that we feel we really are bound to obey. And yet in many cases we would be hard pressed to identify the source of what I call the *normativity* of a law or a demand – the grounds of its authority and the psychological mechanisms of its enforcement, the way that it binds you." Korsgaard, *Self-Constitution: Agency, Identity, and Integrity* (Oxford: Oxford University Press, 2009), 2.

54 Joseph Rouse, "Social Practices and Normativity," *Philosophy of the Social Sciences* 37, no. 1 (2007): 48, http://dx.doi.org/10.1177/0048393106296542.

55 Robert B. Brandom, *Making It Explicit: Reasoning, Representing, and Discursive Commitment* (Cambridge, MA: Harvard University Press, 1994), 18–19.

56 Ibid., 20.

57 Ibid.

58 Rouse, "Social Practices and Normativity," and Rouse, "Practice Theory." See also Schatzki, Cetina, and von Savigny, *Practice Turn*; Reckwitz, "Towards a Theory of Social Practices"; and Stern, "Practical Turn."

59 Rouse, "Social Practices and Normativity," 46.

60 Ibid., 50.

61 Duranti, "Audience as Co-author," 239.

62 Rouse, "Social Practices and Normativity," 50. As Rouse puts it, "what is at stake in those practices is the difference it would make to resolve the issue one way rather than another. But that difference is not already settled, and there is no agreed-upon formulation of what the issues and stakes are. Working out what is at issue in these practices and how the resolution of that issue matters is what the practice is about." Ibid.

63 Ibid.

64 Ibid., 51.

65 Ibid., 52.

66 Ibid., 49.

67 "I have in mind the whole range of phenomena for which it is appropriate to apply normative concepts, such as correct or incorrect, just or unjust, appropriate or inappropriate, right or wrong, and the like." Ibid., 48. Rouse's ideas about a normative conception of social practices are heavily indebted to the philosophy of Robert Brandom. Following Robert Brandom's approach, normativity is located at the level of discursive practices. Discursive practices as actual performances constitute changes of normative statuses – in the sense of social statuses – within the dynamic interactional relations of political agents and processes. For Brandom, normativity lies at the heart of our day-to-day interactions, of our

engagement in the use of language. His conception, therefore, rests on the assumption that "it's normativity all the way down." Brandom, *Making It Explicit*, 623–39.

68 Rouse, "Social Practices and Normativity," 54.

69 Ibid., 52.

70 Brandom, *Making It Explicit*, 20.

71 Jane Monica Drexler, "Politics Improper: Iris Marion Young, Hannah Arendt, and the Power of Performativity," *Hypatia* 22, no. 4 (2007): 3, http://dx.doi.org/10.1111/j.1527-2001.2007.tb01316.x.

72 Young, "Responsibility and Global Labor Justice," 377.

73 "Not infrequently those who assume a stance of rational deliberators in public discourse invoke a narrow image of 'civility' that rules 'out of order' forms of political communication other than prepared statements calmly delivered. On this view, rowdy street demonstrations where thousands of people carry funny or sarcastic banners and chant slogans directed critically at powerful actors, which disrupt normal traffic and force bystanders to listen and look at their signs, go beyond the bounds of deliberative civility. Such an attitude that equates deliberation with orderliness similarly condemns and excludes actions like unfurling banners or displaying symbolic objects with the intent of disrupting bureaucratic or parliamentary routines in order to call attention to issues or positions that those performing the acts believe have been wrongly excluded from a deliberative agenda." Young, *Inclusion and Democracy*, 47. On this point, see also Nicholas P. Low and Brendan J. Gleeson, "Justice in and to the Environment: Ethical Uncertainties and Political Practices," *Environment & Planning* A 29, no. 1 (1997): 21–42, http://dx.doi.org/10.1068/a290021, and Iris Marion Young, "Activist Challenges to Deliberative Democracy," *Political Theory* 29, no. 5 (2001): 670–90, http://dx.doi.org/10.1177/0090591 701029005004.

74 Young, *Inclusion and Democracy*, 178.

75 Elisabeth Conradi, "Inklusion in demokratische Debatten – von der sozialen zur politischen Praxis," in Niesen and Krannich, *Jahrbuch der Heinrich-Böll-Stiftung Hessen e.V.*, 103–10.

76 Drexler, "Politics Improper," 2.

77 Iris Marion Young, "Education in the Context of Structural Injustice: A Symposium Response," in *Citizenship, Inclusion and Democracy: A Symposium on Iris Marion Young*, ed. Mitja Sardoc (Malden, MA: Blackwell, 2006), 98.

78 Drexler, "Politics Improper," 14.

79 Young, *Responsibility for Justice*, 96.

80 Ibid., 111.

81 Young, *Global Challenges*, 179.

8 Institutional Responsibility and Belonging in Political Community

ADRIAN NEER

In a globalizing world, an urgent problem concerns how to structure institutions in order to meet collective responsibilities. These responsibilities, Iris Marion Young has argued, reach beyond personal responsibility:

> Obligations of social justice are not primarily owed by individuals to individuals. Instead, they concern primarily the organization of institutions. Individuals usually cannot act alone to promote justice; they must act collectively to adjust the terms of their relationships and rectify the unjust consequences of past and present social structures, whether intended or not. They need authoritative institutions through which to act collectively.[1]

While a growing literature addresses transnational or cosmopolitan aspects of this problem,[2] Young makes a distinct contribution by defending the self-determination of small, dispersed, or marginalized political communities like Indigenous peoples under the umbrella of the general problem of collective institutional responsibilities. In this chapter, I argue that a key feature of this contribution is the emphasis placed on the importance of relational recognition between political communities. In particular, Young shows how state recognition of the shape of Indigenous political communities is a precondition of their institutional self-determination.

In the first section I describe two distinct positions advanced by Young that bear on the problem of allocating institutional responsibility. In the second section, following a recent article by Jacob T. Levy, I critique Young's deployment of the principle of nondomination to allocate institutional responsibility. In the third section I extend Young's insight that political communities may not have the appropriate institutional means to pursue their interests into a distinction between institutional affiliation and belonging in political community. But when this distinction is advanced, two difficult questions arise. First, how are political communities identified apart from their institutional expression? Second, on what basis should conflicts over claims to institutional authority be adjudicated? In exploring and expanding Young's answers to these questions, I show that relational recognition is a normative imperative, particularly for large national political communities in their relations with Indigenous political communities. In the final two sections I examine the situation of the Tsilhqot'in First Nation in British Columbia. In their attempt to control resource extraction on their territory, the Tsilhqot'in have directly confronted the challenge of presenting their political community's claims apart from the institutions recognized by the state as representative of their First Nation. This example, I conclude, demonstrates the practical importance of the ideal of relational recognition between political communities.

Two Positions Relevant to the Problem of Institutional Responsibility

The basic premises of Young's later work, outlined in *Inclusion and Democracy*, are that inclusion means giving those who are affected by a decision a say in making it, that inclusion furthers democracy, and that democracy furthers justice. This deep commitment to inclusive democratic practice leads to two positions relevant to the problem of how to structure institutions in order to meet collective responsibilities.

The first position is that the threat to democratic voice in an era of globalization should lead us to attempt to match the scope of institutions with the actual interdependencies that exist between individuals and groups. What Young calls "social connection" – the fact that A's actions have B's actions as a background condition, and vice versa – means that A and B have obligations of justice to each other. Out of the thesis that social connection creates obligations of justice arises one of the key research questions of Young's later work: "what is the proper scope of the democratic polity, and how are exclusions enacted by restricting that scope?"[3] This will apply, Young claims, both above and below the level of the sovereign state:

> The scope of a polity ... ought to include all those who dwell together within structural relations generated by processes of interaction, exchange, and movement that create unavoidable conditions of action for all of them.[4]

Below the state, Young criticizes how municipal boundaries in the United States are used to allow wealthier citizens to escape obligations to an interdependent region.[5] Above the state, the current international system is heavily weighted towards the interests of nation states, especially those in the North to the detriment of the South, and towards the interests of corporations. In *Inclusion and Democracy*, she makes several proposals to match webs of interdependence with the necessary institutions, including democratic reform of the UN and its institutions, and "a global system of regulatory regimes to which locales and regions relate in a federated system."[6] These regimes will cover issue areas such as the environment, trade, human rights, and so on, and will "provide a thin set of general rules that specify ways that individuals, organizations, and governments are obliged to take account of the interests and circumstances of one another."[7] Further, on her account the state's "uniformity, centrality, and final authority ... would be seriously altered."[8] Young is thus committed to moving beyond a traditional conception of the sovereign state that can block interference from outsiders, as well as any obligations to outsiders, through appeal to its sovereignty. Institutional responsibility is decentred.[9]

The second position in Young's work relevant to the problem of collective institutional responsibilities is her resolve to recognize the self-determination claims of groups such as Indigenous peoples. Their claims, she insists, are impossible to realize under a traditional understanding of state sovereignty. In order to ensure the "equal right of peoples to self-determination," Young challenges the standard state-centric, Westphalian model that understands self-determination as exclusive jurisdiction for a people within a defined territory, with no obligation to engage with or come to the aid of other peoples.[10] Understanding self-determination on this "noninterference" model is itself responsible for many of the exclusions that borders enact.[11] Young prefers a relational social ontology for groups to definitions that depend on substantive characteristics; "if we abandon the either/or conception of nation," she says, "then the distinctiveness of peoples emerges as a matter of degree."[12] A strength of this account is that a wide range of groups can count as peoples deserving of political self-determination and individuals can more readily conceive of themselves as members of multiple peoples at once.

Because peoples are not and cannot be neatly differentiated according to substantive criteria, but only by degree, sharp distinctions such as those of the non-interference model will be detrimental to the self-determination of many peoples, and do not capture how peoples mix and interact with one another. As a more inclusive alternative, Young draws on feminist accounts of relational autonomy and on Philip Pettit's theory of freedom as nondomination.[13] Pettit argues that the traditional understanding of individual freedom as non-interference is misconceived. It is not interference per se that is objectionable, but the capacity for arbitrary interference that does not consider the interests of those who are potentially interfered with. Institutional arrangements within the state should be designed so as to reduce this capacity for domination. Young describes her extension of Pettit's view from the individual case to that of peoples in these terms:

> Pettit argues that states can legitimately interfere with the actions of individuals in order to foster institutions that minimize domination. A similar argument applies to actions and relations of collectivities. In a densely interdependent world, peoples require political institutions that lay down procedures for co-ordinating the actions of all of them, resolving conflicts and negotiating relationships.[14]

This extension of the ideal of nondomination goes beyond blocking the capacity for arbitrary interference. It also makes the positive claim that the right of self-determination implies an obligation to listen to the concerns of other peoples and come to jointly acceptable resolutions of difficulties.[15] In a globalizing world, where peoples are intertwined to a significant degree, political institutions and other procedural mechanisms must be designed to channel and regulate interactions. Without such institutions and mechanisms, the self-determination of peoples could be compromised by domination. The contrast with the Westphalian world is sharp: rather than inhabiting an exclusive territory in which a nation is not interfered with and has no obligations to other peoples, self-determining peoples are obliged to ensure their relationships with other peoples are nondominative, and to design institutions to meet this end.

In summary, Young is committed to (1) arguing that institutions should be matched to actual webs of interdependence in order to ease structural injustice, and (2) defending the self-determination of peoples and employing the principle of nondomination as a standard for their mutual relations.

Levy on the Right to Exclude

Jacob T. Levy raises an important objection against Young's account.[16] Indigenous peoples, he argues – one of Young's key examples – will need areas of jurisdiction in which they have non-interference rights to ensure that they are not dominated by the state:

> A conception of self-determination such as Young's that lacks [...] legal rigidity and clarity, one that emphasizes negotiation over the question "who holds the rights?" rather than negotiation over how rights holders exercise their rights, unavoidably tends to multiply initial power imbalances.[17]

Indigenous peoples, Levy insists, need the right to exclude on certain issues. Exclusion does not preclude negotiation; rather, one group has the right to make a decision, and then the other can negotiate with the first in an attempt to persuade it to act differently. To make his point, Levy employs a distinction between the scope and degree of authority in making a decision.[18] Scope denotes the range of issues over which a particular jurisdiction has authority. Degree denotes the level of independence the jurisdiction has in making the decision. Levy accuses Young of mischaracterizing the non-interference view as "all-or-nothing."[19] If it was, it would be wholly implausible, but in fact there are many examples of jurisdictions, including those limited jurisdictions under the control of Indigenous groups, which have a high degree of independence to make decisions over a narrow range of issues. Levy asserts that "non-interference, whether in today's international sphere or domestically within a federation, is always a constrained and limited rule. An actor has rights of non-interference *within certain domains* or *subject to certain constraints*."[20] Without some non-interference rights, he thinks Young underestimates how her two positions are in tension, to the potential detriment of the self-determination of Indigenous groups.

More generally, Levy worries that even if a principle of nondomination is accepted as appropriate for normatively evaluating the merits of a particular issue, it will not be a useful decision rule because "rules about jurisdiction ... concern who gets to decide the merits of a question."[21] Without the specification in advance of a jurisdiction that has the authority to make a decision, free from interference from outsiders, including those who will be affected by the decision, the principle of nondomination will simultaneously decide the merits of an issue and the jurisdiction to make that decision.[22] It cannot, according to Levy, function as a decision rule for apportioning political responsibility to particular institutions.

Young noted that her analysis "should not be construed as a proposal for concrete institutional design, but rather as a set of principles that social movements and policy makers should keep in mind in their work."[23] Levy also concedes that Young's general optimism about democratic encounters, and her commitment to not buy stability at too high a price, may speak in favour of a more fluid employment of the nondomination principle, where frequent debates over the proper functions of particular institutions would occur.[24] But a more satisfactory answer to Levy's objection, I argue in the next section, can be developed by extending Young's insight that political communities may lack the institutional means to achieve their interests into a general distinction between institutional affiliation and belonging in political community.

Distinguishing Institutional Affiliation from Belonging in Political Community

In a traditional Westphalian model, the state is the primary mode of both institutional affiliation and belonging in political community. Sometimes, the one-to-one match is approximated: citizenship in the state and national belonging are the individual's primary attachments. But in a globalizing world, there are multiple and overlapping modes of both institutional affiliation and belonging in political community.[25]

Clearly, institutional affiliation is plural in the post-Westphalian world.[26] Regional or supranational institutions like the European Union, other international organizations, Indigenous political organizations, institutions of international law, and transnational civil society organizations exist above, within, or across the state. The case of the EU is an important example of how the jurisdiction of nonstate institutions overlaps with state jurisdiction. As an increasingly powerful regional and supranational institution, the EU treads awkwardly on the sovereignty of its member states. The powers of EU courts and the EU bureaucracy are substantial enough to support the claim that the Union as an institution is already more than an international organization reliant on the delegative authority of its member states. In addition, EU citizens exercise both their home state and EU citizenship.[27] These features of the EU clearly challenge the traditional dominance of the state form in contemporary Europe.[28] As a second example, consider the case of Indigenous political institutions. Indigenous peoples claim self-determination, but their institutions are subject to the authority of the states in which they reside. In many cases, they seek to expand their power in order to more effectively represent their own interests. The claims they raise problematize the division of the globe into mutually exclusive sovereign states.[29]

Institutional affiliation is a formal status, and as such it is relatively clear who is affiliated with which institution(s). Belonging in political community, by contrast, is a more nebulous concept. An individual could belong to a national political community that overlaps with a state, or to an Indigenous political community that overlaps with an Indigenous political institution, or to a supranational political community that overlaps with a regional organization. Or that individual could be a member of a political community that does not overlap with a formal institution such as a state, Indigenous political institution, or regional organization.[30] This multiplicity is unsurprising, given the variety of political communities, the range of reasons individuals may have for identifying with a political community or communities, and the array of criteria political communities might employ to decide who belongs and who doesn't. In the case of Indigenous political communities in Canada, for example, complications to defining their membership include the fact that Indian status has been formally administered by the settler state, the existence of a clash between traditional governance structures and the band system outlined in the Indian Act, and the divide between those living on-reserve and those living in urban areas.

Despite these complications, a method for identifying political communities is needed. As we have seen, Young was keenly aware of the potential mismatch between a community's needs and its institutional means.[31] But her approach to identifying political communities links them to their institutional expression:

> Insofar as a collective has a set of institutions through which that people make decisions and implement them, then the group sometimes expresses

unity in the sense of agency. Whatever conflicts and disagreements may have led up to that point, once decisions have been made and action taken through collective institutions, the group itself can be said to act.[32]

In this formulation, Young addresses the epistemological question of when groups have expressed "unity in the sense of agency." The advantage of the epistemological perspective is that it is silent on what constitutes the political community in question, beyond the fact that it has acted through a particular institution. Ethnic, national, or religious identities are obvious candidates for the basis of political community, but are mired in controversy.[33] Because Young's view avoids direct reference to the potentially controversial constituents of the identity of a political community, it is able to capture the wide diversity of political communities in a globalizing world and allow for the fact that they may act through multiple institutions. For example, Indigenous groups in settler states could act through the legal framework of the state, appeal to the universal framework enacted through the Declaration on the Rights of Indigenous Peoples, or design institutions of their own – from local bands to regional, national, or supranational Indigenous institutions. Thus, Young's view is able to account for the many possible ways a political community may pursue its interests and projects. And, critically, it does not demand a direct link between a political community and a state.

Although the epistemological perspective can allow for the case where political communities pursue their interests through multiple institutional forms at once, it makes the most sense when there is a single institution that a political community acts through. Adapting Young's view to the case where political communities act through multiple institutional forms would require saying which actions a political community takes are more important than others. But how can this be done without falling back into a substantive approach?[34] This difficulty, I think, suggests that a balance must be struck between an epistemological emphasis on identifying political communities through their institutional actions and the ontological question of what makes up a political community.

Young's own approach to political community can be the basis for such an account. In emphasizing its relational nature, Young pushed us to recognize the possibility that diverse political communities may lack the institutional means to achieve their interests, or may use multiple institutions to do so. The need to recognize these possibilities, I argue, is a normative demand for relational recognition that should fall on all individuals as members of political communities, including on national communities when assessing the demands of nonnational political communities.[35]

The need for relational recognition between political communities bears on Levy's objection to Young. Levy, to recall, says that approaches such as Young's "unavoidably tend[] to multiply initial power imbalances." While legal rigidity may be lacking in Young's appeal to nondomination, the benefits of a right to exclude on particular issues should not be overstated. If the shape of an Indigenous political community is misrecognized, the possession of a right to exclude may be a weak bargaining chip in further negotiations with the state. In the following section, I explore how the question of who holds rights may be just as critical as the question of how rights are exercised.

The Tsilhqot'in Nation Case

A long-running court case dealing with the right of the Tsilhqot'in Indigenous political community to control resource development on its traditional territory near Williams Lake, BC, provides an instructive example of the normative imperative of relational recognition. In *Tsilhqot'in Nation v. British Columbia*, trial judge Justice Vickers of the BC Supreme Court ruled on a range of issues, including Tsilhqot'in claims to Aboriginal title and rights. But in order to decide those issues, Justice Vickers faced the prior issue of deciding which political community was the proper holder of both title and rights.[36]

The Tsilhqot'in are a BC Indigenous people comprising six official bands, five of which are represented by the Tsilhqot'in National Government.[37] The Province of BC argued that the Xeni Gwet'in, the Tsilhqot'in nation that launched the original legal action, was the proper rights holder. The Canadian federal government and the Tsilhqot'in themselves argued that the proper rights holder was the Tsilhqot'in Nation, not an individual band as defined by the Indian Act. In essence, the members of political communities such as the Tsilhqot'in are arguing for the use of different criteria than are currently employed to relate institutions to their political communities.

In his decision, Justice Vickers noted that "there is no legal entity that represents all Tsilhqot'in people."[38] Despite this, he argued that

British Columbia places too much emphasis on the notion of a single decision-making body at the time reserves were established. The use of a
small decision-making body for one particular purpose is not necessarily
the hallmark of a community.[39]

Aboriginal title and rights, Justice Vickers concluded, are held by the
Tsilhqot'in Nation.[40] The proper rights holder, in other words, is a political community, despite the fact that it lacks an institution to represent it. To support his argument, Justice Vickers mentions ontological
elements of Tsilhqot'in identity:

> The creation of bands did not alter the true identity of the people. Their
> true identity lies in their Tsilhqot'in lineage, their shared language,
> customs, traditions and historical experiences. While band level organiza-
> tion may have meaning to a Canadian federal bureaucracy, it is without
> any meaning in the resolution of Aboriginal title and rights for Tsilhqot'in
> people.[41]

While Justice Vickers's ruling identifies the Tsilhqot'in political community independently of the institutions that represent it, his reliance
on the "true identity" of this community seems to shade into the substantive approach to political community that Young rejects. And, despite the favourable ruling, the judicial identification of the Tsilhqot'in
raises many interesting questions. What if the Canadian federal government had taken the position of the BC government, and failed to
recognize the Tsilhqot'in community as a whole? What if the court had
ruled differently?[42] The Tsilhqot'in would, in light of the power differential between themselves and the federal and provincial governments,
face a situation where relational recognition of their own, self-ascribed
political community would be lacking.

These possibilities highlight the normative importance of relational
recognition. Although the court may not be the best forum for achieving relational recognition of nonnational political communities, in some
cases it is the only option available. Further, an alternative, Westphalian
approach that elides the distinction between institutional affiliation
and belonging in political community is unlikely to resolve conflicts
over relational recognition. Indeed, it is likely to cover them over, as
the position of British Columbia in *Tsilhqot'in Nation* demonstrates. An
advantage of Young's approach, I conclude, is that it demonstrates that

state recognition of the shape of Indigenous political communities is a precondition of their institutional self-determination.

The Prosperity Mine

As Young would surely maintain, however, emphasizing the importance of the question of who holds rights need not minimize the importance of how these rights are exercised. Again, the struggle of the Tsilhqot'in to resist resource development on their traditional territory provides an example of why this is the case.

On November 2, 2010, a controversial application by Taseko Mines Ltd to develop a copper-gold mine, called Prosperity, on land the Tsilhqot'in Nation considers its traditional territory, was rejected by the federal government.[43] In support of his decision, Environment Minister Jim Prentice cited environmental concerns and the impact on First Nations. However, Prentice could have ruled that the economic benefits of developing the mine outweighed environmental concerns and the infringement of aboriginal rights. Indeed, the provincial government's own environmental assessment, although criticized by environmental groups, had concluded the project should go ahead.[44] And, although it resulted in the rejection of the mine proposal, the federal environmental assessment process did not include the Tsilhqot'in as a full partner. Instead, the Tsilhqot'in were left to air their concerns in front of a process that was already underway, and which ultimately left the decision on approval in the hands of a federal minister.

The recent spike in gold prices has improved the economics of the project, and Taseko has submitted a revised application.[45] The Tsilhqot'in now face the prospect of pleading their case in front of a new environmental assessment panel.[46] Some factors point in the direction of approval for the new mine proposal. For example, the mine is strongly supported by BC premier Christy Clark.[47] The likely approval of a revised Prosperity application demonstrates the challenges facing First Nations in resisting resource development applications on their traditional territories. Resource development proposals like the Prosperity mine affect traditional aboriginal lands and rights, and First Nations need control over their traditional lands in order to be self-determining. But First Nations are left with few options other than pleading their case in front of environmental assessment panels or pursuing court action.

Clearly, a right to exclude the Prosperity Mine from its territory would give the Tsilhqot'in a powerful bargaining chip in its relationship with Canada and British Columbia. Further, in *Tsilhqot'in Nation*, the roots of this right to exclude were outlined in Judge Vickers's declaration of aboriginal title.[48] While the BC Court of Appeal has rejected parts of Judge Vickers's ruling, an appeal to the Supreme Court of Canada is likely.[49] A declaration of aboriginal title from the Supreme Court of Canada would undoubtedly strengthen the hand of the Tsilhqot'in and other BC First Nations, and greatly reduce the discretion the government has to approve resource development projects that infringe aboriginal rights and title. But resolution of conflict over how resource development applications are processed, I suggest, must involve both relational recognition of Indigenous political communities by the state and the distribution by the latter to the former of a measure of jurisdictional authority over the approval of applications. Institutional self-determination – in this case a right to exclude resource development activity – is made meaningful by state recognition of the shape of Indigenous political communities.

NOTES

1 Iris Marion Young, *Inclusion and Democracy* (Oxford: Oxford University Press, 2000), 250.
2 David Held, *Democracy and the Global Order* (Stanford, CA: Stanford University Press, 1995); James Bohman, *Democracy across Borders* (Cambridge, MA: MIT Press, 2007); and Nancy Fraser, *Scales of Justice* (Cambridge: Polity, 2008).
3 Young, *Inclusion and Democracy*, 6.
4 Ibid., 197. Young argues that globalization is advancing the entanglement of individuals in webs of interdependence with distant others, and that these entanglements raise the issue of how institutions should be structured to match this interdependence. There is a problem of institutional responsibility as long as there are webs of interdependence that create obligations of justice, and there is a mismatch between existing patterns of institutional organization and these webs of interdependence (ibid., 246–51).
5 Ibid., chapter 6.
6 Ibid., 267.
7 Ibid.

8 Iris Marion Young, *Global Challenges: War, Self-determination and Responsibility for Justice* (Cambridge: Polity, 2007), 35.

9 Ibid., 33–4. By contrast, Nagel argues that justice is possible only within the bounds of the state. The state is the ultimate location of institutional responsibility, and the responsibilities of other institutions will be derivative on the responsibility centred in states. Thomas Nagel, "The Problem of Global Justice," *Philosophy and Public Affairs* 33, no. 2 (2005): 113–47. John Rawls developed a similar position. His *Theory of Justice* located institutional responsibility in the major institutions of a society's basic structure partly on the basis of the assumption that society was "closed" – that individuals lived full lives within it. When the bounds around domestic society were removed in the later work *Law of Peoples*, "peoples" became the actors who agree to a law of peoples to govern their mutual relations. This extended Rawls's earlier claim about institutional responsibility from the domestic to the international sphere. John Rawls, *A Theory of Justice* (Cambridge, MA: Belknap, 1971), and Rawls, *The Law of Peoples* (Cambridge, MA: Harvard University Press, 1999).

10 Young, *Global Challenges*, 6–7. While Indigenous peoples seek self-determination, they often do so without calling for their own sovereign, territorial state. Young, *Inclusion and Democracy*, 255–6. Also see the essay "Hybrid Democracy: Iroquois Federalism and the Postcolonial Project," in Young, *Global Challenges*.

11 Young, *Global Challenges*, 44. One of the roots of Young's view is her concern with social differentiation and structural inequality. She attempts to include marginalized groups by making room for their voices as a window on and resource for negotiating the needs of inclusion in contexts where some interests have more of an effect on decisions than others. For example, structural inequalities attend gender, race, and class in domestic society, and similarly, structural inequality attends the bordering of more powerful states into sovereign territories in relation to less powerful states. See Young, *Inclusion and Democracy*, chapter 3.

12 Ibid., 253.

13 Philip Pettit, *Republicanism* (Oxford: Oxford University Press, 1997).

14 Young, *Inclusion and Democracy*, 260.

15 Thanks to Nancy Bertoldi for discussion on this point.

16 Jacob T. Levy, "Self-determination, Non-domination, and Federalism," *Hypatia* 23, no. 3 (2008): 60–78.

17 Ibid., 72.

18 Ibid., 69.

19 Ibid., 68.

20 Ibid., italics in original.

21 Ibid., 70.

22 Ibid.

23 Young, *Global Challenges*, 32.

24 Levy, "Self-determination," 75.

25 To deny the distinction – to say that institutional affiliation automatically overlaps with belonging in political community – may miss (1) horizontal challenges to traditional state models, such as secession, (2) vertical challenges, such as federalism or regionalism below the state level and supranationalism above it, (3) communities based explicitly on choice, and not fate, such as transnational NGOs, and (4) cases where there is a mix of identity and territory, such as Indigenous groups that distinguish themselves through an Indigenous identity and a claim on territory. See note 2 for contemporary defences of the Westphalian view.

26 Rainer Bauböck writes that political boundaries have: "[a] dual nature ... which demarcate jurisdictions over territories or persons ... Theoretically, there are two possible mismatches between territorial and membership boundaries: political communities can be distinct and separate with regard to their membership, while their territorial jurisdictions overlap, or, conversely, polities may have territorially separate jurisdictions while their membership overlaps." Rainer Bauböck, "Political Boundaries in a Multilevel Democracy," in *Identities, Affiliations, and Allegiances*, ed. Seyla Benhabib, Ian Shapiro, and Danilo Petranović (Cambridge: Cambridge University Press, 2007), 92. Bader and Engelen argue that comparative institutionalism should play a larger role in political philosophy because of the need to incorporate pluralism in a way that state-centred accounts make difficult. Doing so, they argue, would reveal the "hidden institutional assumptions" of much of current theorizing. Veit Bader and Ewald R. Engelen, "Taking Pluralism Seriously: Arguing for an Institutional Turn in Political Theory," *Philosophy and Social Criticism* 29, no. 4 (2003): 379.

27 Thomas Risse, *A Community of Europeans?: Transnational Identities and Public Spheres* (Ithaca, NY: Cornell University Press, 2010).

28 Jürgen Habermas, *The Postnational Constellation*, trans. and ed. Max Pensky (Cambridge, MA: MIT, 2001), and Habermas, *The Crisis of the European Union*, trans. Ciarin Cronin (Cambridge: Polity, 2012).

29 Taiaiake Alfred, *Peace, Power, Righteousness: An Indigenous Manifesto* (Don Mills, Ontario: Oxford University Press, 1999), and Duncan Ivison, Paul Patton, and Will Sanders, eds., *Political Theory and the Rights of Indigenous Peoples* (Cambridge: Cambridge University Press, 2000).

30 This could be because a political community lacks effective institutional representation. The *Gastarbeiter* in Germany, for example, live in an indeterminate state with respect to their membership in the German

polity. Germany's citizenship and naturalization laws, as Benhabib notes, changed from a *jus sanguinis* basis to *jus soli* only in 1999. Seyla Benhabib, *The Rights of Others* (Cambridge: Cambridge University Press, 2004), 156. With this change, some of the issues facing the *Gastarbeiter* have been resolved. But a sense of belonging in the national political community remains a challenge.

31 Young discussed the situation of American Indigenous peoples at length, and also applied her theory to the conflict between Israel and the Palestinians. See the essay "Self-determination as Nondomination: Ideals Applied to Palestine/Israel," in Young, *Global Challenges*.

32 Young, *Global Challenges*, 50.

33 Brian Barry, "Statism and Nationalism: A Cosmopolitan Critique," in *Global Justice*, ed. Ian Shapiro and Lea Brilmayer (New York: New York University Press, 1999), 12–66.

34 Thanks to Nancy Bertoldi for raising this objection.

35 Schouls suggests that the relationship between the state and Indigenous political institutions should be "seen as the outcome of a process in which Canadian governments recognize their federal obligation to create political space for Aboriginal communities so that they can develop and express their communal identities in freedom." Tim Schouls, *Shifting Boundaries: Aboriginal Identity, Pluralist Theory, and the Politics of Self-government* (Vancouver: UBC Press, 2003), 129–30.

36 Tsilhqot'in Nation v. British Columbia, 2007 BCSC 1700, para. 437–72.

37 Although there are six official bands, Justice Vickers identifies seven Tsilhqot'in political communities. "The Tsilhqot'in National Government, a federally incorporated legal entity, only represents five of the seven Tsilhqot'in communities." *Tsilhqot'in Nation*, para. 456.

38 Ibid. Additionally, Justice Vickers noted that the case was launched by the Xeni Gwet'in and drew primarily on historical and ethnographic evidence from their community.

39 Ibid., para. 451.

40 Ibid, para. 470.

41 Ibid., para. 469.

42 Thanks to Nancy Bertoldi for raising this objection.

43 Wendy Stueck, "Ottawa Vetoes Controversial Prosperity Mine Project in B.C.," *Globe and Mail*, 3 November 2010, http://www.theglobeandmail.com/news/national/british-columbia/ottawa-vetoes-controversial-prosperity-mine-project-in-bc/article1783048/ (accessed 13 August 2011). The Prosperity application raises a series of related issues such as the jurisdiction of the provincial government, case law on Aboriginal title, and the BC

treaty process. See Dwight G. Newman and Danielle Schweitzer, "Between Reconciliation and the Rule(s) of Law: *Tsilhqot'in Nation v. British Columbia*," *U.B.C. Law Review* 41 (2008): 249–76.

44 British Columbia Environmental Assessment Office, "Prosperity Gold-copper Project Assessment Report," 17 December 2009. For an example of the criticism levelled at this report by environment groups, see West Coast Environmental Law, "Lessons from the Prosperity Mine Environmental Assessment," 2010, http://wcel.org/resources/environmental-law-alert/lessons-prosperity-mine-environmental-assessment (accessed 6 July 2011).

45 Taseko's description of the "New Prosperity" mine can be found at http://www.newprosperityproject.ca/ (accessed 13 August 2011).

46 The Tsilhqot'in, along with other interested parties, have noted that the new proposal was originally judged by Taseko to have a more damaging impact on the environment than the proposal that has already been rejected.

47 Ian Bailey and Justine Hunter, "Christy Clark Presses Harper over Rejected Mine Proposal," *Globe and Mail*, 15 March 2011, http://www.theglobeandmail.com/news/national/british-columbia/bc-politics/christy-clark-presses-harper-over-rejected-mine-proposal/article1943610/ (accessed 13 August 2011).

48 Kent McNeil, "The Meaning of Aboriginal Title," in *Aboriginal and Treaty Rights in Canada: Essays on Law, Equality and Respect for Difference*, ed. Michael Asch (Vancouver: University of British Columbia Press, 1997), 135–54, and McNeil, "Reconciliation and Third-party Interests: *Tsilhqot'in Nation v. British Columbia*," *Indigenous Law Journal* 8, no. 1 (2010): 7–25.

49 William v. British Columbia, 2012 BCCA 285.

Contributors

Nancy Bertoldi, Associate Professor, Department of Political Science, University of Toronto

Genevieve Fuji Johnson, Associate Professor, Department of Political Science, Simon Fraser University

Loralea Michaelis, Associate Professor, Department of Politics and International Relations, Mount Allison University

Margaret Moore, Professor, Department of Political Studies, Queen's University

Adrian Neer, Doctoral Candidate, Department of Political Science, University of Toronto

Tanja Pritzlaff, Research Associate, Department of Political Science, University of Bremen

J.L. Schiff, Assistant Professor, Department of Politics, Oberlin College

Melissa S. Williams, Professor, Department of Political Science, University of Toronto

Index

15–16, 78–101; commodified power and, 13, 43, 44, 45–50, 56, 59; conflicts in models, 15–16; constitutive power and, 14, 44, 45, 50–2, 59; cosmopolitan theories of, 28–32; disciplinary power and, 14, 45, 52–4, 56, 57, 59; forward-looking, 9, 14, 65, 126, 128, 140n34; hybrid model of, 15–16; individual responsibility compared to, 5–7, 19; intergenerational, 103, 105, 114, 115, 118; legal responsibility compared to, 5–7, 19, 20n5; liability model compared to, 122, 125–9, 136–7; moral responsibility compared to, 5–7, 19, 20n5; nonvoluntary association and, 6–7; performances of, 17, 123, 124, 126, 135–6, 137; pluralist account of, 79; political obligation compared to, 4–5, 19, 19n2, 19n3; preinstitutional, 29, 30, 32; refocusing of, 4, 14; relational conception of, 14; Smiley and, 19n4; social contract model of, 15, 89–93, 94, 96; state-centered theory of, 18; symbolic power and, 14, 44, 45, 54–8, 59; territorialization of, 51; Young's conception of, 124–31. *See also* collective responsibility; fiduciary model; institutional responsibility; liability model; power-responsibility relationship; social connection model; traditional account; utilitarian approach

Political Responsibility Refocused title, 4

Political Theory and International Relations (Beitz), 29, 38n3

Polizeistaa, 85

pollution, 12, 27, 108

poor countries, 26, 47

positions, of privilege, 43

positive/negative duty distinction, 22, 23–4, 32, 39n10

post-Westphalian views, 18, 149

poverty: global, 12, 21, 26, 29, 32, 114; poor countries, 26, 47

power: Arendt's concept of, 50–1, 61n2; commodified, 13, 43, 44, 45–50, 56, 59; constitutive, 14, 44, 45, 50–2, 59; disciplinary, 14, 45, 52–4, 56, 57, 59; Hobbes and, 50, 52, 85; misrecognition and, 43–4, 49, 54, 55–8; production of subjects and, 45, 52–4, 57, 60; relational conception of, 14; symbolic, 14, 44, 45, 54–8, 59; violence compared to, 45, 61n22

power-responsibility relationship, 42–62; Bourdieu and, 14, 44, 45, 54–7; capabilities approach, 44, 45, 58–9, 95; conclusion, 59–60; Foucault and, 14, 44, 45, 52–4, 55, 56, 85; overview, 13–14, 44–5. *See also* crises

practice theory, 17–18, 124, 133. *See also* political practices

predatory lenders, 47

preinstitutional responsibility, 29, 30, 32

privilege: exclusion and, 51–2; false presumption of impartiality and, 67; positions of, 43; structural injustice and, 130; sweatshops and, 13

procreate, obligation to, 105

production, of responsible subjects, 45, 52–4, 57, 60

Prosperity Mine, 154–5, 158n43,

shared institutional framework, 29
shared responsibility: backward-
looking, 41n35; defined, 14, 128;
genocide and, 33, 97; May's view
of, 41n35; social connection model
and, 32–4, 127; structural injustice
and, 124; Young and, 59
Shaw, William, 104, 105–6
Singer, Peter, 23, 104–5
slavery, 112
Smiley, Marion, 19n4
social connection, autonomous
development and, 64–6, 75n7
social connection model, of political responsibility: assessment/
critique of, 22, 35–8; Canadian
decolonization and, 93–7; cosmopolitanism and, 10, 14, 22, 32, 93;
deontological model compared
to, 16–17; description of, 8–9;
forward-looking political responsibility in, 9, 14, 65, 126, 128,
140n34; future generations and,
16–17, 109–18; global justice and,
10, 11–12, 21–41; interdependencies and, 47, 145–6, 147; legal responsibility and, 9; liability model
and, 9, 13–14, 43, 47, 48–9, 65–6,
139n23; main features of, 127–31;
moral responsibility and, 9; as
shared connection model, 21, 22,
38n2, 114–15, 115, 118; structural
injustice and, 9–10, 11, 13–14, 17,
33; traditional model compared to,
9, 12–13, 22–8, 37–8. See also global
justice; structural injustice
social contract model, 15, 89–93, 94,
96, 101n28
social norms, racialized, 111–12
social practices, 17, 135, 142n67

solidarity, 5, 15, 95–6
South, global, 32, 71–2, 146
South Africa, truth and reconciliation commissions, 88
sovereign power, 50, 52, 85
sovereignty, Westphalian, 18, 69, 70,
71, 72, 146, 147, 149, 153, 157n25
special obligations, 22, 115
state-centered theory, of political
responsibility, 18
stateless people, 48, 51
Steiner, Hillel, 109
structural inequalities, 33, 65, 110,
112, 113, 115, 117, 156n11
structural injustice: defined, 10,
60n8; difficulty in responding to,
49–50; liability model and, 122;
privilege and, 130; production
of, 122–3; remedy for, 10; shared
responsibility and, 124; social connection model compared to, 9–10,
11, 13–14, 17, 33; structure (term)
and, 33. See also social connection
model
subjects: docile, 53, 54; militant, 54;
production of, 45, 52–4, 57, 60
subordination, gendered relations
of, 67
sui generis obligation, 85, 100n17
surplus labour theory, of value
conception, 24, 39n12
sweatshops, 8, 12, 13, 33–4, 43, 46,
47, 48, 53, 54, 63, 71–2, 113, 124–5,
130, 135
symbolic power, 14, 44, 45, 54–8, 59

talent, 30
Tan, Kok-Chor, 29, 30
Taseko Mines, 154, 159nn45–6
teleology, 104, 106